P9-CEU-784

MAX FRISCH

Modern Literature Monographs

MAX FRISCH

Carol Petersen

TRANSLATED BY CHARLOTTE LA RUE

Frederick Ungar Publishing Co.
New York

Translated from the original German and published by arrangement with Colloquium Verlag, Berlin. New material and revisions for the American edition were prepared by the author.

Second Printing, 1979

To Edgar C. Reinke,
a most honored friend

For the convenience of the reader, all titles of German works are given in English. For German titles and translation data, please see the bibliography.

Contents

Chronology

1911: 15 May: Max Frisch is born in Zurich
1924–30: Attends the Kantonal Realgymnasium
1930–33: Studies German language and literature at the University of Zurich
1933–36: Works as a journalist
1934: Publishes his first novel, *Jürg Reinhart*
1936–40: Studies architecture
1937: *Answer from Silence* is published
1939–40: Serves in the Swiss army
1940: *Leaves from a Knapsack* is published
1942: Marries Constanze von Meyenburg
1943: *The Difficult Ones* is published
1944: Works on *Santa Cruz*. Opens an architect's office of his own
1945: *Bin, or The Journey to Peking* is published. March: *They Are Singing Again* is produced for the first time in the Züricher Schauspielhaus
1946: March: *Santa Cruz* is produced for the first time in Zurich. The first version of *The Chinese Wall* is produced in the fall. Frisch visits Germany for the first time after the war
1947: Begins to design the swimming pavilion Letzigraben, completed in 1949. Notes under the title *Diary with Marion* are published. Frisch travels to Czechoslovakia, Italy, and Germany
1947–48: Works on *When the War Was Over*

1949:   8 January: *When the War Was Over* is produced
         for the first time in Zurich. Frisch writes the first
         version of *Count Öderland*. Travels to Germany
         and France
1950:   Travels to Spain. *Diary 1946–1949* is published
1951:   *Count Öderland* is produced for the first time in
         Zurich
1952–53:   Lives in the United States and Mexico
1953:   *Don Juan, or The Love of Geometry* is produced
         for the first time in Zurich and Berlin, simultane-
         ously, in May. "The Firebugs" appears as a radio
         play
1954:   The novel *I'm Not Stiller* is published
1955:   A new version of *The Chinese Wall* is produced
         in Berlin. Frisch gives up his profession as an archi-
         tect
1956:   Makes a second trip to America. *Count Öderland,*
         the second version, is produced in Frankfurt
1957:   The novel *Homo Faber: A Report* is published
1958:   *The Firebugs* is produced in Zurich in a program
         with *The Great Rage of Philip Hotz*. Wins Georg
         Büchner Prize and Literature Prize of the town of
         Zurich
1959:   Frisch is divorced from first wife
1961:   *Andorra* is produced for the first time at the Zü-
         richer Schauspielhaus. The third version of *Count
         Öderland* is produced in Berlin. Frisch moves from
         Switzerland to Rome
1963:   *Andorra* is produced in New York City
1964:   A *Wilderness of Mirrors* is published
1965:   Frisch moves from Rome to Ticino in southern
         Switzerland. Is awarded Schiller Prize of Baden-
         Württemberg
1967:   The play *Biography: A Game* is published
1969:   Frisch marries Marianne Öller. Travels to Japan
1970–71:   Lives again in the United States. Is guest lec-
         turer at Columbia University, New York City

A Meeting
with Max Frisch

On a lovely spring day in 1971 I went to Columbia University in New York City to meet Max Frisch, who was teaching there. In the classroom I met not a famous writer, not an authoritarian schoolmaster, but an intensely human man.

I saw the face of a man who is equally at home in both realms: in practical life as well as in intellectual precincts. Intellectual ferment and restlessness are expressed by the high forehead and the eyebrows, but a compensating composure is communicated through the smoke that rises from his ever-present pipe.

Frisch's face is one that belongs to the twentieth century, a face that lacks any trace of the *fin-de-siècle* mood. There is no relationship between its expression and that of a Kafka or a Rilke, whose features so clearly reflect the fact that they are men making the transition from an individually oriented epoch to a group-oriented one, whose faces reveal a questioning, anxious striving toward a personal understanding of their own inner worlds. Frisch's face belongs, rather, among the genera-

tion of men that has lighted up the middle third of our
century with their strong, intelligent radiance, oriented
more to the world as a whole than to the continual contemplation of the inner psyche: the generation of a
Camus, a Brecht, a Zuckmayer, a Steinbeck, a generation of antinihilists. His face reveals his spiritual alliance
with that generation. Not only did Frisch feel deep admiration for Brecht; even after Brecht's death, he continues to be preoccupied by his work and to feel genuine
fondness for it.

The encounter between writer and young people
is often impressive, sometimes even gripping. Its effect
is often lasting, because today's young people prefer to
get guidance and advice from the writer rather than
from traditional mentors such as teachers, fathers, min-
isters, let alone leaders in society and industry.

Frisch, however, does not claim deeper insight into
matters, does not assume the role of a prophet. And
when his students praised his work as deeply philosophi-
cal, when they said that he had taught them how to see
banal day-to-day events with more perceptive eyes, and
thus how to better tolerate and understand them, he
gently turned aside the reverent admiration.

Frisch told me later that he likes to come to America, that by teaching here he modifies his world view
according to what he learns from Americans. He feels
he profits from communication with young Americans,
whom he finds especially open-minded and less preju-
diced than the young people in many European countries. Teaching and learning are for him reciprocal ac-

tivities; at the age of sixty he feels learning is a significant part of his life.

In the important lecture "Our Arrogance toward America," Frisch not only criticized the prejudice against the New World held in many circles of Europe's cultural bourgeoisie but also repudiated it for the very reason that it *is* a prejudice. His personal experiences of living in America taught him to recognize the "father-son relationship" between Europe and America as something determined by nature and therefore necessary and beautiful, an interaction from which the whole world can derive advantage. He believes that man as world-citizen, one who is genuinely concerned with problems lying beyond the borders of his own country, was born in America. In contrast to Switzerland, America to him is not an organism that "has become," but one that "is becoming." Frisch considers Europe important, to be sure, along with his love for the entire world, but Europe alone "is not humanity, not culture."

"While writing I don't defer to anyone," he said. (He made this point apropos of the fact that he sometimes endows his characters with very unusual names.) He may have been justifying the fact that his novels are so "private," a word he interprets in the sense of "referring to interpersonal relationships," not as an adjective describing only his own life. A human being in his relationship with other humans is for Frisch a "model of experience," a pattern whose presenting is the writer's vocation. In so doing the writer must of necessity reveal much of himself, although not directly as a sort of au-

tobiographical kind of writing. Frisch likes to use alle-
gories, which he thinks better reflect historical or whatever kind of real facts. He has been sometimes criticized
for this attitude, yet this does not distract him from his
writing approach. Problems merely political as well as
religious do not preoccupy his mind when it comes to
presenting heroes of world history. He wants to show
them first of all as human beings with all their positive
and negative features; mere abstractions are almost excluded from his works. He has consciously developed
literary techniques for writing "exclusive private plays,"
techniques that enable him to crystallize human fates
whereby these fates even increase in grandeur. He has
little interest in presenting a comprehensive picture of
our contemporary world.

The Swiss writer Max Frisch is today one of the
most highly regarded living writers in the Western
world. He has been equally successful in the fields of
drama and fiction, each form inconspicuously but convincingly supplementing the other. His plays, more than
his novels, may have exerted more influence in German-
speaking countries because they have reached more people. Reality and fantasy are deliberately intermingled in
these dramas, reinforcing one another to carry out carefully developed ideas. Frequently based on very simple
facts, a spectrum is created that gives the theater what
belongs to it. But whatever the variety of effects, his
underlying ideas remain easy to grasp. Is this a result of
the two vocations to which Frisch felt himself committed during a long period of his life: the work of an
architect and that of a writer? Architectonic structural

laws, quite typical of the asymmetrical architecture of the twentieth century, may be found in many places in his literary work, too.

Theater is to Frisch a world of wonders that never fails to cast him into enchantment. What distinguishes a theatrical production from a novel is that it takes place in front of an audience, that, one might say, it "acts interpersonal" itself. When you read a play, you experience it as a literary work; it is not until it is performed that it becomes theater. "Genuine theater is what proves to be intense, which, of course, sometimes can become embarrassing," Frisch said. Frisch cares as much about the sensuous elements of life and experience as he does about the spiritual ones. The "interpersonal element" for him is not restricted only to one's knowing *about* another person, but is inseparably linked to one's experiencing the bodily presence of the other person. What makes theater so precious to him, more dear than movies and television, is the fact that only there can one "feel quasi-magically the body of other human beings." So theater for him is not only a "moral institution" (as it was for Schiller) or not only a "place of education" (as it was for Brecht) but also—as he says—an "erotic institution." That eroticism is a basic impetus of creativity is self-evident to him.

That Frisch is Swiss gives him satisfaction and pleasure, because that very accident of birth placed him in a better position to serve as an advocate of objective judgment and justice during World War II, when the divided nations were seeking mutual annihilation. He ranks as one of the greatest writers of the postwar period because he presented the events of war-torn Europe without prejudice or partisanship, and, through the medium of his characters, fairly allotted both human greatness and human weakness to the warring nations. Self-satisfaction, of which the Swiss are frequently accused, is foreign to his nature. In his role as citizen of a neutral "small country," he believes that he has more mental freedom than is held by citizens of the powerful states—"the greatest possible scope for individual thought, because the small state, because it is powerless, cannot become an image before which one has to sacrifice his integrity." This theme of the perniciousness of the "image" is basic in Frisch's work, and I shall examine it in my discussions of *When the War Was Over* and *Andorra*.

In order to be more objective, more just, he as a Swiss has a special need for the non-Swiss in Switzerland. The term "over-foreignization," often used in Switzerland in deprecation of the numerous tourists and workers who arrive there from other countries, does not imply an unfortunate situation to him. On the contrary, it means continual stimulation, which increases "dissatisfaction with stagnation" and reduces the tendency to dwell in the past, which he finds undesirable.

"Let's resume our conversation another time, maybe when you come to the Tessin one day," Frisch said to me when we parted. While saying this he pulled his perennial short pipe out of his pocket. Then the labyrinth of the New York subway swallowed each of us into different directions. I do indeed hope to continue my dialogue both with Frisch and with his works.

The excursion that lies before us, through Frisch's life and work up to the present time, is the fruit of my acquaintance with him up to this point. I am fully conscious of the danger involved in such an account of the works of a writer still in our midst, at the peak of his creative powers. Nevertheless, I hope this study will be a profitable introduction of a great playwright and human being to American readers.

—CAROL PETERSEN

Valparaiso University, Indiana, 1971

1

In the
Shadow
of Tradition

.

Time does not change us,
it only develops us.—M.F.

Zurich, the largest city in Switzerland, although not its capital, is the background against which the crucial, formative years of Max Frisch's youth ran their course. A city famed for the beauty of its natural surroundings and the richness of its artistic life, loved by all the world, a rare and happy symbiosis of sedate, bourgeois tradition and moderate worldliness, Zurich provides an appropriate atmosphere that continues to have a beneficent effect for a creative life—as it did for the boy who was born on 15 May 1911 in the suburb of Hottingen.

Max Frisch's ancestors came from Austria, from Württemberg in Germany, and from Switzerland. His father, an architect, made it possible for Max and his brother to complete the gymnasium. Max, the younger of the two, had an overwhelming interest in the theater from an early age. His mother, née Wildermuth, was the daughter of a painter, who had once been the director of an arts and crafts school in Zurich. Coming from a bourgeois-artistic milieu Max was the only member of his family to scale the peaks of artistic achievement. In 1930 Max passed his final examination at the gymnasium, more for his parents' sake than for his own. At this time he had already decided on the precarious career of a writer. While still a student, he first tried his hand at drama writing. The results were a play entitled "Steel," a domestic comedy, and a play about the conquest of the moon. With the fine unconcern of youth—he was sixteen at the time—he sent them to Max Reinhardt in Berlin, who returned the manuscripts two months later with detailed criticism and encouraged him to continue writing.

In his *Diary 1946–1949*, in which he gives accounts of his early youth, Frisch presented the stages and turning points in his development that provide a deep insight into his career. His own summing up of this period cannot be improved upon by the pen of another. After his graduation from the gymnasium, Frisch studied German language and literature for two years at the University of Zurich. Years later, in the park at Versailles in 1948, he wrote in his diary the following lines, a beautiful statement of self-understanding in retrospect:

Going to the University was unavoidable. I remember two strange years, which I spent in lecture halls and, with almost as much stimulation, in corridors—always expectant, lonesome, hasty in judgment, insecure, usually entangled in a secret love. The poems I wrote were never successful. Pure philosophy, which I approached with real ardor, showed me only my own lack of intellectual power. My major field was German language and literature. Actually, other courses seemed to me closer to the mystery of life. Certainly one owes to an unsatisfying period of time more than the dissatisfied student realizes. The growing feeling, however, that everything one learns is without a central focus, that what is called a university is a warehouse of haphazardly stored knowledge—all this may be a completely genuine emotion, perhaps even an insight; but at the same time it also served as a welcome excuse for one's own weakness in academic work.

Frisch very clearly outlines in the *Diary* the intellectual starting point of his later creative work. He sees art as the "regulator" to the claims science has on our age. Only in the reconciliation of the two (art and science) to the claims made on them by the times, and in their mutual reconciliation to one another, does he find the deeper meaning of art as well as of science.

When he lost his father in 1933 (he was twenty-two), he was confronted for the first time by the immediate worries of existence. Completely responsible for himself and jointly responsible for his mother, he had to look around for a way to earn a living. The profession of journalism suggested itself, since it offered the young man, hungry as he was for experience and knowledge, an opportunity to get acquainted with a wide variety of places in the world. In his "Autobiography" (covering the years to 1947), a separate chapter that he inserted as a centerpiece in the *Diary 1946–1949*, Frisch wrote:

As a journalist I wrote about what was assigned to me: parades, lectures about Buddha, fireworks, seventh-rate cabarets, fires, swimming contests, spring in the zoo. I refused only to cover cremations. All this provided some not unprofitable education. The world-championship hockey games took place in Prague. I made myself a reporter and started off, after the purchase of my first suitcase, with cash resources of a hundred francs. [By using the word "reporter" Frisch means to make a distinction between the reporter, who simply tells the reader objectively what is happening, and the journalist, who makes comments on what he watches.] The journey, my first to a foreign country, led me farther with every article published at home or in Germany—to Hungary and back and forth through Siberia, Bosnia, Dalmatia; and there, having soon made friends with German emigrants, I spent a whole summer, sailing around the coast for days, unencumbered by any obligations, ready for any adventure that turned up. That, then, is my real memory of youth.

Frisch imparted a good deal of this genuinely youthful intoxication with life to the young characters of his early works. He was to continue to follow this pattern as every line he has ever written is flavored by his own experiences. This makes the body of his literary work compellingly believable, often disconcertingly so.

In 1934 Frisch's first book appeared, the novel *Jürg Reinhart*. Is it a coincidence that the name of the hero is the same as that of the young naturalist in Gottfried Keller's *Sinngedicht*? Undoubtedly not, since Frisch has acknowledged, and still does, his debt to Keller, and has called *Green Henry*, Keller's great *Bildungsroman*, his "best father." His strong inner affinity to this nineteenth-century Swiss novelist is frequently apparent in Frisch's life and work. Both of them, each in his own century, represent a breaking away from the circumscribed life of the Swiss people, who are always conscious of their rights and obligations as citizens to their local communities and to their country. By Swiss standards, Keller and Frisch each led an extraordinary life, but at the same time they (and many of their fellow countrymen as well) knew that it is only the extraordinary, in a higher sense, that sustains order in human life. Each, at a crucial point in his life, burst through the boundaries prescribed by birth and upbringing and traveled for years outside Switzerland. The jet plane, which makes it possible to span continents with ease, is the only difference between the experiences of the twentieth-century Frisch and those of Keller in the previous century. Frisch's ardently experienced years of travel have basically the same meaning as did Keller's years in Munich, Heidelberg, and Berlin.

Jürg Reinhart treats the problem of the relationship between artist and bourgeois in a manner related to that of Keller's *Green Henry*, but adapted to a new age. The subject matter of both novels is the striving of a young man of a bourgeois family for self-fulfillment in an anti-bourgeois way of life. In *Green Henry* a lonely, introverted young man is brought up in a bourgeois world full of exciting persons and things. Yet, he cannot find the right goal in life for himself. He sets out into the world of adventure, living a rather self-centered life with little concern for his family, especially for his mother. In the first version of this novel Green Henry dies repenting painfully the neglect of his mother, who had sacrificed for him most of herself. While in the first version this novel had been a story told in the third person, Keller later changed it to one in the first person. In the second version moreover, Henry returns to a life of humble order, and, as an official in the municipality of his hometown, he finds self-fulfillment at the service of his community and the community of men.

In Frisch's *Jürg Reinhart* basically the same structure and principle are maintained. Jürg Reinhart, much like Green Henry, experiments with a variety of professions and goes through a number of love affairs at different places and in different countries in order to find his true ego and his proper vocation in life. In the end he finds, just as Green Henry did, that his striving to become an extraordinary man in his field has been in vain. Realizing that he must resign himself to a life of devotion in duty, he becomes a gardener.

Jürg Reinhart and the novella *Answer from Silence*

(1937), set in the mountains, are the two published early works that Frisch destroyed, along with everything else he had written up to about 1937, in a book burning by his own hands. In the autobiographical sketch in his *Diary 1946–1949* he wrote:

Once I tied up everything that I had ever written, including my diaries, and burned all of it. I had to make two trips into the woods, there were so many bundles. I remember that it was a rainy day, and the fire was constantly going out because of the dampness. I used up a whole box of matches before I could depart with a feeling of relief, but I also left with a feeling of emptiness. For two years afterward I did not seriously break my secret vow never to write again.

In 1938 in Zurich he was awarded the Conrad Ferdinand Meyer Prize for literature.

Shortly before the time of the book burning life seemed to be pushing Frisch in an entirely different direction—that of architecture. A girl whom he wished to marry said that he would have to make something of himself first. Frisch became aware that he had lived, up to that time, with too much trust in chance, that it was time for the early years of roaming and blind confidence to come to an end and for him to make more conventional plans. In 1936 he decided to become an architect. A friend offered to support him for the next four years, and Frisch, now twenty-five years old, matriculated at the Eidgenössische Technische Hochschule. Of this decision he wrote: "What especially moved me to take up this profession was what was different in it, the nonliterary, the tangible, the manual work, the material shape.

Only the actual building, the materialization of my own designs, would finally show whether or not I would fail in the second attempt, too" (quoted from the autobiographical chapter in the *Diary*).

How greatly this field of study was to benefit Frisch's later literary work is clearly evident today. In all his writings—particularly in his three great novels, *I'm Not Stiller*, *Homo Faber*, and *A Wilderness of Mirrors*—he applies the architectural laws of space organization to both the exterior structure and the interior supports, a matter that strikes and fascinates even the uninformed reader. The *Diary* gives important evidence as to how the two professions, which Frisch pursued simultaneously for years, supplemented one another and enriched and enhanced his total life work.

But even before Frisch had earned his diploma in architecture, his life took another radical turning. In 1939 he was drafted into the Swiss army for defense duty at the border. It amounted to "something more than five hundred days of service, mostly in Tessin, later · in Engadin." To this period we owe Frisch's return to his writing.

His well-received diary of army life, *Leaves from a Knapsack*, was first published in 1940. In it, Frisch's observations of life at that time and his stated attitudes toward it contain the whole man in embryo. It is abundantly clear throughout the book that Frisch, little as he sympathized with the Nazi philosophy, felt no kind of hatred or bitterness, though such attitudes would have been understandable.

Leaves from a Knapsack is impressive, not only because of Frisch's complete freedom from prejudice at a time that was characterized by bitter feeling, but also because it reveals the beginning of the line of development that was to remain unbroken from *Leaves from a Knapsack*—the first book he was to find acceptable to himself since the destruction of his two early works—to *A Wilderness of Mirrors* in 1964. His entire work to date is characterized by a broadening and deepening of his understanding of the world but not by the contradiction or even occasional reversals of position that mark the work of so many writers of stature of our century (for example, of Ernst Jünger or of André Gide, who even elevated the inclination to such reversals to the status of a virtue). Frisch's attitude toward his work rests on his subjective acceptance of the whole of life, not on the mastery of an isolated, arbitrarily selected section of life. Without pathos or vanity he has subordinated other attitudes to a concern for all his fellowmen. We are impressed not only by his unqualified desire for objectivity, but even more by the broad scope of the objective discoveries resulting from this desire. This trait, too, makes him the legitimate descendant of Gottfried Keller. Frisch continues a distinguished tradition, while he renews and refreshes it in the spirit of the twentieth century.

It perhaps required the horrifying spectacle of World War II, with the development of the atomic and hydrogen bombs, to make Frisch remeditate life as a whole. Insofar as man needs to be frightened at times in order not to fall victim to self-righteous lethargy, Frisch may have grasped, even at the beginning, the

threat of the war but faced the apparently preordained
disasters with equanimity. For change in life, under
whatever circumstances, seemed to be helpful for Frisch
not to fall into complacency and quietism. Change in
life, resulting in a man's more mature personality, is always necessary in Frisch's opinion. Change is good even
in days when, as he wrote, "you feel like a miserable bug
that is brushed aside by a large and petulant hand just
when, after long years of trying, you think you have finally discovered a way out."

In *Leaves from a Knapsack* we meet the soldier on
the other side of the border as a fellow human being,
and the Swiss soldier as a world citizen. This attitude is
all the more noteworthy when we recall the situation
in which Switzerland found herself in 1939—in danger,
as a small weaker country, of being attacked and swallowed by the "colossus to the north," as had already
happened to Austria and Czechoslovakia.

Momentarily a strong national feeling seems to erupt
when Frisch writes: "We will love our fatherland and
defend it." But he immediately adds the qualifying
phrase, "but never worship it," thereby setting a clear
line of limitation to any form of nationalism to which
one has not submitted voluntarily in a period of national
emotional upheaval. Wartime obliges Frisch, even more
urgently, to express solidarity with his fellowmen. He
writes:

And it is good that we have no choice. After all, who wants
to be excluded in this hour? Who could continue his regu-
lar work in quiet and pleasure, while others stand guard in
the mountains and rub their blue hands together? And
who could still follow his own wishes now, when there are

only women and old men and children to stand in the fields and bind the ripe sheaves, now when girls are volunteering in the hospitals? There is no vacation from the time! Not even at home.

Then the day came when Hitler invaded Poland and, as Frisch wrote, the question that he had asked himself so often in the past years, "whether there is sense in taking a position against a superior force, simply evaporates."

Primarily Frisch experiences contemporary political events as they occur in time in purely human terms, in terms of how they affect the individual. History, on the other hand, i.e., political events evaluated and made into something abstract, he considers on the whole phantomlike.

In the end, what grips the poet in Frisch is the wartime confrontation with death, which brings men involuntarily closer together than they are in everyday life in peacetime. To become conscious of the transitory nature of all material possessions signifies a new stage of maturing. As Frisch most convincingly puts it in *Leaves from a Knapsack*:

There is a great deal to be said for it, this condition where you abandon everything that does not fit in the knapsack, that you cannot carry hour after hour on your own back. So much is left behind that only recently you considered to be indispensable; and yet you keep one thing, always and everywhere, whatever happens: the indelible memory of people to whom you are attached, and the belief that things will continue in the outside world if you are in order inside yourself, the belief that the human heart, always and everywhere, even now is more real than so-called great events.

The value of *Leaves from a Knapsack*, that which
still makes it so much worth reading, lies not alone
in the fact that it helps us understand the frame of
mind of a neutral people at the beginning of the great
world holocaust, nor merely in the fact that they reveal
Frisch as a sensitive landscape artist (the glowing colors
of Tessin are painted as beautifully as if the words were
pastels). Their special worth is clearly expressed in the
book itself in Frisch's statement of the insight he gained
through his military experience: "People of a small
state, what in the world is there for us to conquer if not
the expanses of the heart, the purity and nobility of a
state of mind?" As if it were a pledge made to himself,
Frisch has remained faithful to this idea up to the present day.

In 1940 Frisch was granted a leave of absence in
order to take his state architectural examination in
Zurich. "A young architect who helped me at the draw-
ing board and prepared lunch for me became my wife.
We got married after we had built our first house together." The student was not the girl he previously had
wished to marry, but Constanze von Meyenburg, the
daughter of a Zurich professor from a well-to-do, respected family. They were married in July 1942. There
were three children from the marriage, a son and two
daughters. By 1953, however, marital difficulties had
started to arise, and in 1959 they were divorced. In 1969
Frisch married Marianne Öller.

In 1942, Frisch was working on the novel *The Difficult Ones*, a new version of the *Jürg Reinhart* he had
destroyed years before. *The Difficult Ones*, published in

1943, was still a typical work of youth, charming but not quite full-grown. Charming in its hero, Jürg Reinhart, in his vehement denial of ordinary, bourgeois life patterns, in his various attempts to live on his own; and at times voluptuous in the vivid colors with which it depicts the natural beauties of Switzerland. It is immature in Jürg Reinhart's final casting off of his life, since he does not succeed in really getting a hold on life or, to phrase the idea in a way more typical of Frisch, he does not succeed in achieving an identity.

The young painter Jürg Reinhart is the type of artist we are familiar with from the great German *Bildungsroman* (novel of development). We have encountered him in the figure of the early Green Henry (in the novel of that title) and then, more fully developed, in the artists as portrayed in the early works of Thomas Mann. With his attitude focused on the absolute, his belief that, as an individual, he must always lay claim to superiority and special prerogatives, he is confronted with the conventional bourgeois world, a rock on which he is finally wrecked. The theme is old; the manner in which Frisch treats it is completely new and independent.

The novel treats the problem of the artist versus the bourgeois by means of sophisticated love relationships. The whole action dramatically opens with Reinhart's question to Yvonne, the young wife of an archeologist, living in a conventional marriage with which she is already bored. He asks her if she knows who she really is. The question inevitably leads to Yvonne's separation from her husband, since it results not only in her

being attracted to Reinhart, whom she feels to be
stronger than she, but also in her taking the first step
toward finding herself. The description of the first time
the lovers are alone together is filled with pearls of late-
romantic writing:

> They stopped to rest at a country inn. . . . The ordinary
> working day, filled only with the buzz of a fly and the cluck-
> ing of chickens outside, surrounded them with the festive
> mood of young truants. All questions, those without an-
> swers, retreated behind a curtain of solacing happiness. . . .
> Clouds of happiness, akin to sorrow, embraced and carried
> the afternoon hour, . . . the unexpected feeling of com-
> munion that, like fate, had been lying in wait in this coun-
> try inn, the knowledge that they had come together.

But this "knowledge" proves, in the end, to be painful illusion after longed-for fulfillment. For, to the extent that the encounter helps Reinhart to find himself
as an artist in his environment, it isolates and consumes
him. For Yvonne and Jürg Reinhart there is only one
summer of happiness, a high point in the life of each.
Then, forced to obey their mutually irreconcilable natures, they separate. Reinhart continues to be a sleep-
walker, as though he has learned nothing. It is Yvonne
who dismisses him, lets him fall back again into himself. Is it cruel fate or a merciful providence that causes
it to happen in this way? Jürg Reinhart himself gives us
the answer:

> "It's good this way! I love life with all its raging discords.
> . . . Devotion, giving, dreams, happiness. You can hardly
> imagine how two people could be closer to one another.
> And then, like a purgatory—twisted passions, jealousy, re-
> sentment. That it is over, simply over, . . . that in all this

there is a deep, cool, universal bliss, a humility, a recognition, an acceptance—yes, that all this can be . . . as cruel as it is splendid! There was no other way to go but forward, we had to go through it. Through ourselves, through the world, through all the delights and pains of life!"

Still, in the depths of his being, the demands of real life remain strange and incomprehensible to Reinhart, while Yvonne marries a man who is well able to take care of her and to offer her things every reasonable woman could wish for. Yvonne alone knows that the child she is carrying is Reinhart's.

Reinhart's attempt to fit into bourgeois life after he loses Yvonne is, from the beginning, destined to fail. His relationship with Hortense, an officer's daughter, is broken off as soon as she finds out what Reinhart's background really is: that he is the illegitimate child of an alcoholic and a woman who committed suicide. His final attempt to attain self-acceptance through the simple life of a gardener is the third and last phase of a shattered life from which, for Reinhart, there is only one escape—suicide. But life itself continues: in Reinhart's and Yvonne's son, who becomes a friend of Hortense's daughter. With a glimpse of the young pair rowing on the lake, Frisch leaves us with a glimpse of ongoing, unending life.

With this romantic work, Frisch wrote himself free of his youth. The book was read by Kurt Hirschfeld, stage director of the Züricher Schauspielhaus, who felt that, judging from the very natural and lifelike dialogues in this novel, Frisch might well be able to write a play and encouraged him to make a first attempt in this direction.

26 *Max Frisch*

But before taking on this challenge, Frisch was faced with another task, which was to be of great importance to his financial security. As winner of a competition in which eighty-two architects took part, he was chosen to build a large public swimming pavilion in Zurich. In his own architectural office, which he kept until 1952, he drew up plans for the bathing establishment Letzigraben, built in the years 1947–49. His *Diary* gives a clear account of the progress of his architectural work and of the joy he took in this service to the people. He also wrote about the construction site, which was one that had been a gallows hill centuries before and where the workmen, during the excavations that had to be undertaken, found skulls of humans. As in a daydream, Frisch ponders in these passages the transitoriness of life.

The first notes about the building are dated August 1947. In October of the same year the *Diary* gives further information, always with an emphasis on what was being brought to light from the broken, excavated earth, in an almost poetic synopsis of the ages and fates of men: "Here the Russians fought the French. The bricks of a Roman villa are widely scattered over the gallows hill, butcher's tools, family gardens. . . . For the time being it is I who work my will in this small spot of earth, general of five hundred and thirty thousand square meters."

The pleasure of building was not exhausted for Frisch with the planning and measuring, nor even with the cleanly executed manual work. The social, the human element, which is part of the creation of every building, also affected him strongly, since, as a creative man, he always sought to encompass, even in the smallest object, the whole of life. For him, a building made by hand is a living contrast to the great dangers that mechanization and automation hold for life today. In his *Diary* Frisch clearly explains his concept of the craftsman's everlasting proper task:

The cabinetmaker always appears to me as the epitome of the artisan, in contrast to the worker; his natural raw material, wood, does not come from a factory. . . . People who work with metal are different; what comes into their hands is already fabricated. . . . The worker says that he worked on the indoor swimming pool, the artisan says that he made the railing there. The difference also exists in the way they act toward the architect. The artisan feels he is a full colleague, and our conversation is usually fruitful.

From these lines we see clearly how friendly and cooperative Max Frisch is, how he responds to others as man to man, with the firm knowledge of the necessity of all occupations for the mutual good.

Today the swimming pavilion Letzigraben is probably the only extant building by Frisch. In the course of time, the writer in him proved to be more demanding than the architect, but he never entirely gave up this intensively experienced contact with concrete reality.

A "reverie in prose" is what Frisch himself called his next work, which was written in 1944 and published in 1945: *Bin, or The Journey to Peking*. The little book is sheer poetry. The pipe-smoking Bin (almost all of Frisch's heroes smoke pipes) is Frisch's alter ego. Because at some time every man stops to think not only

about his own life but about life in general and all the
unfulfilled longings that it brings about, it happens that
at the beginning of the journey of Bin and Frisch to
Peking, Frisch says:

At least half of life has passed, and secretly we begin to be
ashamed in the presence of the adolescent whose expectations have not been fulfilled. I drifted toward a longing that
is not worth mentioning, since (we know and smile at it)
it returns every year, a matter of the seasons, a March
homesickness for new people, to whom you yourself would
be new, so that it would be enriching to converse pleas-
antly, to consider many things, even to become inspired—a
homesickness for the first long conversation with an unknown woman. Oh, to wander out into the night, untrou-
bled by any restrictions! We will certainly not escape from
any such restrictions that lie in ourselves.

Here, for the first time in Frisch's creative writing,
he separated life and dream in order to reunite them
more closely at the end. For life and dream are not po-
larities in Frisch's mind but a unity. The dream is the
most real reality of life, not opposed to it. But often we
forget our dreams. Frisch admits in this highly poetical
story that he, too, had forgotten time and again his
dream, personified by Bin. But dreams never release us
completely. They do not allow us to have a life without
them, and they finally convince us that they are real,
that without them we would not be fully human beings.
In the end we cannot do anything but follow our dream,
unconcerned whether or to what extent it can be fulfilled, unconcerned by how little the longed-for aims it
produces in our minds are in accord with the circumstances of our real life, that is, to what extent our ideals
can come true.

Thus the journey to Peking represents man's ultimate goals in life, which not every human being has the
energy and will power to strive after all his life. What
in this case is called Peking, far behind the Great Wall
of China, is called, in a famous play of our time, Godot.
That which Samuel Beckett personifies or deifies in
Waiting for Godot has become a place in Frisch's story,
but in both cases it is a magnet for unfocused longing,
the attainment of which would allow us to reach beyond ourselves. We are not always aware of our longing;
it is only the everlasting stimulus to our highest possible
fulfillment. What the poets have always known, the psy-
chologists have in the meantime confirmed. Peking, the
world of the Far East, is to be understood here as nothing but a fairy-tale dreamland, with no connection to
geographical or historical facts. With the help of Bin,
who one spring evening entices the narrator away from
his family supper table to a dream journey, Frisch con-
quers the nostalgia that the civilization of our century
has brought about in so many people. The world of the
Far East, less concerned with and less accustomed to
modern civilization, for that very reason seems less
alienated from the world of the dream. That is what
makes Frisch say, as a conclusion, that forgetting or ig-
noring our dreams leads to a dehumanized form of life,
to an antlike form of life, which has become more and
more typical for the man in the Western world. Frisch,
as the narrator, in *Bin, or The Journey to Peking* puts
it in the following words:

We live like ants back there in the West. . . . Each soul
is like a snow shoveler, it pushes a continually growing, always larger and more troublesome heap of unsatisfactory

life before it, becomes tired and old. The result is this, that one has merely existed, and still we are all determined to postpone death as long as possible. We invent expedient after expedient, but for all our cleverness and industry, we still work like ants.

Bin materializes in the flesh to confront Frisch, who comes to realize that Bin is the best in us, which we so frequently ignore, the dream in us, which we gradually allow to fade in order to comply with reality. This work sounds like a melancholy requiem for the Western world, almost a renunciation of it. But a clear contrast follows when the same narrator at the very end of his story raises hope for himself and, by doing so, for his readers, too. He says that the ancient land of the dream will survive and that there would no longer be any creativity among men if that land would ever perish.

With this small, faultlessly beautiful "reverie," Frisch laid the foundation for the whole future structure of his writing, which was never to lack faith in the ultimate regeneration of Western man. It is the kind of hope that is an integral part of every form of Christianity. Paul Tillich perceived it as the link between theology and culture, and Frisch, without professing explicitly any religion, has woven it into his entire work. He has never strayed from this hope. As he continues to place other characters before us, we see their fates worked out in an inseparable web of thought and action, reality and dream, in an especially fine interplay of temporal and spatial units.

2

The Counter-World of the Stage

The scene of the play is always the human soul—M.F.

Out of the same material—that is, out of the "dreaming" from which the prose poem *Bin, or The Journey to Peking* was created—came also Frisch's first writing for the stage, the romantic drama *Santa Cruz*. Written in 1944, the same year *Bin* was written, it was produced for the first time in March 1946, by Heinz Hilpert, the master director of poetic theater in Zurich. As far as its sources are concerned, *Santa Cruz* appears to show the influence (of which Frisch himself was probably not aware) of Hofmannsthal, of whom the reader is continually reminded. But the hand of a member of the younger generation can also be clearly traced, although there is almost no direct reference to contemporary life.

Santa Cruz is a late-romantic play, par excellence. Its theme is the Then and Now of love and how they join in the human heart for eternity. It tells the story of a woman and her relationships with two men—a traditional story in this sense. In the reminiscing of seven happy days that had been lived seventeen years ago, the past is brought to life. It is a contrast between a family manor with its snow-covered walls and a far-away place in the southern hemisphere with its colorful and unwalled, wide-open sides. It dramatizes the difference between being sheltered in a permanent home and being homeless—conditions that trouble not only us who live in this century, but that are characteristic of human life in general.

It is also a play of the suspension of time, in which the rich world of "outside" merges without break into the equally rich world of "inside." Nowhere is the basic tone of all Frisch's further writing sounded more clearly than here: that of the presence of eternity in the moment. Elvira, the leading female character in *Santa Cruz*, lives constantly under the spell of the wandering scholar Pelegrin, whom she followed, longing for adventures, to Santa Cruz, a symbolic place in a far-away country where she fulfilled with him her dream. (In this play Santa Cruz is no more restricted to the geographical concept than was Peking in the story of Bin.) Yet, she is brought back by her husband, a cavalry captain and a man of order, to his manor and thus again to a world of security. Elvira, however, does not stop leading a double life—the one in the reality of her marriage and the other in her world of dreams and adventures. One day, Pelegrin, old and wise now, takes refuge with the couple in their manor and finally dies there. Although to Pelegrin marriage appeared as a "coffin of love," to the captain it seems the most exalted form of living—to bear human loneliness together and lovingly. Only among people of true inner freedom and delicacy can such a relationship among three persons become wonderful, a relationship that in ordinary life would lead to jealousy and thus to a banal tragedy of marriage.

The captain is a romantically enhanced version of Hauswirt, Yvonne's husband in the novel *The Difficult Ones*. The captain is a nobleman in the deepest sense of the word. Pelegrin, from a spiritual point of view, is no less so. Both are noble men, as each recognizes the necessity and meaning of the other for the beloved woman who stands at the center of their lives. Thus the captain can say of Pelegrin that he liked meeting this man who led his "other life"; he does not, even for one single moment, think bitterly of this other man for loving his wife as much as he himself does. Perhaps all men, in their imagination, have an ideal they try to live up to, an ideal embodied by someone who lives in a truer way the style of life that he would like to live.

In the end Pelegrin is nothing but the captain's alter ego, and the relationship of the play to the story *Bin* is evident. The captain knows how much richer Elvira has become because of Pelegrin, how much greater her harmony with herself, and it is for this reason that Elvira can tell Pelegrin that her marriage is a truly happy one—even though Pelegrin may smile a hundred times about marriage.

"There is something miraculous about marriage. When we were married then, seventeen years ago, I did not know how very much, how honestly I would be able to love him. One must get acquainted with each other, as we did, before one falls in love. I almost didn't deserve a husband such as he."

In his program notes for the premiere of *Santa Cruz*, Frisch expressed unequivocally his conscious use of the intermixture of times and places that alone makes it possible to reveal human fate:

For it is only when a Then and a Now meet in our experience, only when the repetition helps us to see it, that we realize we obviously have a fate, a cross that must be taken up, a *crux*, or *cruz*, to use Spanish. The Then and the Now: both together comprise the Always that is allotted to these three people.

Frisch called his second work for the stage, *They Are Singing Again*, an "attempt at a requiem." A lyrical-religious play, it was produced for the first time a year before *Santa Cruz,* in March 1945 at the Züricher Schauspielhaus. In it Frisch entered, however reluctantly and warily, the political issues of the time. He wrote in his *Diary 1946–1949:* "The play sprung not from a deliberate intention to lecture the German people but simply from the need to get rid of my own distress." It does not present actual events, but in it the war dead rise again. In some concluding remarks (which Frisch in most cases adds to each of his dramas when published) at the end of *They Are Singing Again* he states emphatically:

The scene where the action takes place always proceeds from the spoken word. . . . For throughout it the impression of a play must be maintained, so that no one will compare it to the actual happening, which was atrocious. We did not see it with our own eyes, and we must ask ourselves whether it is proper for us to speak of it at all. The only circumstance that perhaps can justify our speaking out is this: that we, who have not experienced it with our own bodies, may be freed from the temptation to carry out any revenge. There are scenes that must always remind us of a distant sadness, even if these scenes happened only under the compulsion of such dreams as haunt everyone who has lived through these times. Others will think differently.

At the core of the play are twenty-one slain hostages, men whom Karl, a German soldier at the Eastern Front, had been ordered to shoot before the action of the play starts. The question of the Why of this deed does not leave him in peace. When the curtain rises we hear the voices of the men, who sang up to the moment of their death, as they reverberate in Karl's obsessed mind. The action begins when a Russian priest is commanded to bury the corpses and to be silent about everything he has seen and heard. Out of fear the priest complies, and Herbert, Karl's commanding officer, despises him for that. Then Karl tries to drive home to Herbert the fact that if the priest had never met the German soldiers, he would never have become involved in such a criminal complicity. To save their own lives, most men are able to do things that under normal conditions they would refuse to do, but mortal terror such as Herbert and his fellow officers spread can turn even priests into criminals.

At the end of this scene, in which the question of guilt is raised so pressingly, Herbert orders Karl to shoot the priest, too. But Karl refuses and, instead, runs away. When he arrives home safely, he is overcome by what has happened and tells his father about it. His father tries to persuade him that he has done no wrong, that this is wartime and military orders have to be carried out without pangs of conscience. But for Karl there is no refuge in using obedience as an excuse—obedience cannot be an excuse for murder. He is convinced that responsibility cannot be taken from us even in wartime. Feeling that he has acted against his ethical principles, a highly sinful behavior that can be atoned for only by death, Karl hangs himself.

This scene in particular contains strong echoes of a scene in Wolfgang Borchert's *Outside in Front of the Door,* in which Corporal Beckmann throws back at his former colonel the responsibility for his eleven soldiers who were killed in a scouting raid. Both plays are typical expressions of the mid-twentieth century. No personal experiences of Frisch are utilized in the creation of this play. But it shows most convincingly that Frisch, even as an onlooker, a Swiss, was most deeply involved, simply as a brotherly neighbor, in the political events of the years 1939 to 1945. He juxtaposes accusation and defense, guilt and atonement, always expressing these ideas in the speeches of his characters without ever taking upon himself the role of judge. His high ethical position, in this particular play and in general, is always revealed adequately by the work itself. Thus it is no longer necessary for him to draw special attention to it.

In the fall of 1946, the same year in which *Santa Cruz* was produced, Frisch's *The Chinese Wall* was also produced. A revised version of the play was produced in Berlin in 1955. Frisch labeled this play a "farce," but it would be wrong to interpret this designation in the sense of the medieval farce. It may be that this carousel-like presentation of slices of world history was thought of by Frisch as being only a farce. It encompasses everything in the way of scenic and technical means to shape a whole world passing in review, to make the truth Frisch has discovered even clearer. When we consider this profusion of scenes and stage devices, which, when effectively presented, carry the audience along, it is "total" theater that makes its appearance. Masks, pantomime, choreography—all are present. Indeed at times masquerades are such independent elements that one might almost think the play could be presented as *théâtre de mime*.

The symbolism of *The Chinese Wall* has been in-

terpreted as expressing a final entreaty, warning mankind of the consequences of a possible atomic war. It is
a magnificent allegory in which all laws of time and
space are suspended in order to project the ideas of the
omniscient dramatist who, in this play, becomes almost
a visionary. Using examples of powerful dictators, such
as Hwang Ti, the builder of the Great Wall of China—
his faith that the wall could "bring time to a halt" was
sadly misplaced—and by showing leaders such as Caesar,
Philip II, and Napoleon, the play reveals the dangers
that threaten mankind from those whose highest principle is power. The character, whom Frisch calls "Today's Man" (der Heutige; in the first version Today's
Man is called Min Ko), and through whom Frisch himself speaks, can protest against the total power of
Hwang Ti only by means of his intellect and by wearing the disguise of a fool's cap. Completely powerless
against the representatives of power, he is still the one
who really knows, who has learned from the course of
world history, and who never wearies of holding before
the great and powerful the mirror of their deeds, though
they themselves never doubt the rightness of these
deeds.

In conversation with Napoleon, Today's Man says:
"The next war, which we claim is inevitable, will be the
last."

Napoleon asks: "And who do you think will win?"

Today's Man replies to this: "No one . . . you cannot imagine that, Your Excellency, I know. But it is so.
The great deluge can be engineered. . . . We are faced
with a choice—will there continue to be a human race

or not? . . . But if we decide that there shall be a human race, it means that your way of thinking and making history is now out of the question. We can no longer afford a society that regards war as inevitable, this is clear."

Frisch's attitudes and the manner in which they are presented, the highly effective theatrical qualities of the play, and the unusual and vivid combinations that Frisch presents on the stage are all very impressive. But *The Chinese Wall* is a pessimistic work. Freedom is only in the realm of the spirit; for, in the real world, the possessors of power end up by doing the same things over and over again. Everything remains as it was before, and nothing beyond debunking has happened. It is only a grandiose demonstration of what was fated to happen, ironically emphasized when Hwang Ti himself places a golden chain around the neck of Today's Man, the representative of the intellect. The intellect as decoration but not as an agent that controls power—this appears to be its position now and forever. Only the lovers, Today's Man and his sweetheart, Mee Lan, are more true, more real and unambiguous in the end, but the strength of their hearts cannot change the course of history. Frisch does not want to arouse hopes that might in the end turn out to be deceptive. And it may be that his pessimism has more to offer than a comforting optimism, which would leave people to their emotional and intellectual inertia.

The drama *When the War Was Over*, written in 1947 and 1948, was produced for the first time in Zurich in 1949. (In 1962 Frisch deleted its third act "because

it did not carry the theme forward, and merely dated
the play.") In this play Frisch attacked more directly
than before the subject of the fate of humanity, which
had become the most important question of the first
confused years after World War II, especially in a Germany that was both outwardly and inwardly ravaged.
Frisch succeeded in presenting again, more convincingly
than ever, the old theme of guilt and expiation, bril-
liantly relating it to the special command as given in the
biblical injunction "Thou shalt make unto thee no
graven images."

Frisch learned of the actual event on which he
based the action of the play while visiting postwar Berlin in 1947. His *Diary* recounts in brief form, almost
word for word, his host's account of "a case from the so-
called Russian time." In the play individual features of
the case were changed and dramatically enriched to em-
phasize the relationships of the characters to the time,
but essentially Frisch followed the actual events.

In the center of the action stands a woman. She is
called Agnes, a name that means innocence and purity,
as Frisch expressly mentions in his notes to the play.
She is the wife of a former Nazi officer who had partici-
pated in the massacre of Jews in the Warsaw Ghetto
and who has escaped from Russian captivity. At the
time of the play's action, Russian soldiers occupying
Berlin have taken up quarters in the rooms of their
house, and Agnes is trying to hide her husband in the
basement. She is invited to join the Soviet colonel in
social evenings. So that she will be better able to protect

her husband should the need arise, she gains the colonel's favor by accepting even his sexual overtures. When the colonel learns from a Russian-Jewish soldier about the past of Agnes's husband, he leaves Agnes and the house rather than turn her husband over to the military police. Thus the genuine love relationship that had blossomed between Agnes and the Soviet colonel, although neither understood the language of the other, ends.

In this play Frisch wants to show that by true human feelings all kinds of prejudices can and must be overcome: there is no such thing as the typical German, the typical Jew, the typical Russian. Under all the accidental exterior features lies hidden something more essential and general: the mind and heart of a human being, which ignores, again and again, in the encounter of two human beings, the accidental exterior features for the sake of humanity itself. Frisch's drama *When the War Was Over* is, as he said, the story of a "great exception." The "image"—the idea one irrevocably accepts for everyone one sees in that category—is in opposition to dynamic development and change. Yet it is development and change that are the true laws of life, which alone are able to enrich and refine the human being. The word "image" (*Bildnis*) in this sense makes its first appearance here as a leitmotif in Frisch's work. We will meet it frequently from this point on. An attachment to something immutable is, for Frisch, unnatural and inhuman, and is at its worst when it leads to a categorizing and a labeling of the human being. For him the command to make no graven images is a command to re-

spect equally the "living and inexpressible" in every individual, and the actual events of a particular time must
not weaken this command.

When the play was first presented in Zurich on 8
January 1949, the Swiss audience was so disturbed that
a fracas in the lobby ensued. Although hardly con-
ceivable in a country where well-behaved forms of social
intercourse are still so much more general than in most
other European countries of our contemporary world,
the Swiss audience revolted here, which was quite
understandable at that time. They felt that Frisch had
gone one step too far, that he was on his way to ex-
cusing the war atrocities of the Nazi government and
thus to becoming a "devil's advocate" for Hitler's Germany. Frisch's aloofness from indicting just one nation
had been mistaken for a condonation of the terror
caused by one nation. The German public was later to
show itself more receptive than the Swiss—maybe, in
fact, believing that Frisch was more understanding of
their historical guilt than he actually was.

In 1947 Frisch wrote in his *Diary*:

What fascinates me in this case is that it represents an exception, something special, a living contradiction to the
rule, to prejudice. Everything human is individual. Overcoming of prejudice; the only possible way of overcoming
it, one that makes unto itself no image. In this special case,
facilitated by the lack of a common language. It would
hardly have been possible if Agnes and the Soviet colonel
could have met each other in speech, and then had had to.
Language as the vessel of prejudice! What could bind us
together has turned into the opposite, the fatal separation
through prejudice. Speech and lies! The monstrous paradox

—that people can be closer together without speech. And it seems to me important that it is a woman who provides rescue by overcoming the separateness. The woman, experiencing more concretely, in a better position to accept an individual human being as such and not bury him under a stereotype. She goes to the Russian, an enemy, with a weapon under her dress. Since they cannot understand one another, they are forced to look at each other, and she is able really to see, to see the individual man, really to become, to be a person against a world that is obsessed by stereotypes, against an era when speech has become unholy, not a human language but a language of broadcasters and newspapers, a language that is inferior to the dumbness of animals. . . .

This excerpt incorporates the whole Frisch. I would call it one of the finest passages in the *Diary*, not least because it shows Frisch's courage in rejecting all thinking and feeling of the majority. Anyone who remembers the events, and their causes, of the first postwar years in Germany finds in Frisch a man who had the courage to look into himself and refuse to be misled by the slogans of the powers of that time. He fought resolutely against any form of prejudice. His struggle reached a new height in *When the War Was Over*. He fights even the prejudice apparently justified by events—in this instance, the prejudice long held against Russians as a result of what was believed to have been Russian brutality during the Berlin occupation (and yet the intoxicated victoriousness of invading troops turning into brutality is a phenomenon as old as the world). Beyond the action in this drama we discern a man of higher insight, one with a poet's sense of justice that is capable of seeing a state of affairs as it really was.

Frisch gained this perception of the annihilating effect of prejudice during his many journeys through the devastated lands of the postwar world, and since then he has taken it up again and again in his work. The hate propaganda of the Nazis instilled, over many years, in millions of people the image of the Jew as evil, as a perverter of the human race. In the postwar years in Germany this image, this prejudice, seemed to be transferred to the Russians—a chain of self-perpetuating misunderstanding and lack of understanding that would of necessity lead to further injustice and murderous inhumanity. In *When the War Was Over* an individual, documented episode, transformed into creative literature, served to sound a warning.

Frisch's next work, revised three times and staged since 1961 in its final version, was *Count Öderland*. It is his most controversial play. From the original production in Zurich on 10 February 1951, to the first German production in Frankfurt on 4 February 1956, to the revival in a new version in Berlin on 25 September 1961, it has provoked the most diverse reactions.

In the *Diary* we find a preliminary draft of this drama, which Frisch was to describe as a *Moritat in zwölf Bildern* (morality play in twelve scenes). Once again he has written a tale of romantic rebellion—it has the yearning for faraway places as well as the protagonist's abrupt rejection of all his ties and values, his flight from the narrowness of normal middle-class life—in this case, the life of a prosecuting attorney, a life in which one is especially committed on the side of law and order. The seven narrative scenes in the *Diary* are, as it were,

the first rehearsal of the subsequent dramatization of
the material. Frisch gives us a hint of the protagonist's
world view in the last of these scenes when the protagonist says: " 'I could never kill a human being, but a customs official, yes, a policeman, yes. . . .' " This detail in
the *Diary* is developed further in the drama, in which
Frisch allows his protagonist to become a criminal.
Öderland believes he can force his way to power and
despotism with an axe and find self-fulfillment as a sort
of a superman. The thought may come to mind that
this is an allegory of Hitler, but Frisch has expressly denied this interpretation. He intends Öderland's position
to be understood in a broader, more general way: as that
of an educated man, dissatisfied, despairing of the values
and responsibilities brought about by this very education, and finally abandoning them because he believes
that, without them, he can attain a freer and truer life.

In presenting the profusion of wrong that the protagonist then commits, Frisch goes so far as to devise sensa-
tional effects such as are commonly found in crime
stories. The real literary substance, which time and
again breaks through strongly in certain scenes, is therefore less effective and credible. As a whole the play
seems to be without unity and, in the end, unsatisfying.
The entire action is strangely schizophrenic.

The first scene presents a clear point of departure,
completely convincing as it reveals the prosecuting attorney's state of mind in two dialogues, first with his
wife and then with the housemaid. He holds these conversations the night before he is to present the state's
case in the trial of a murderer who killed a janitor with-

out motive. A doer without relationship to his deed, a doer without regret—the case is similar to that of Meursault in Camus's tale *The Stranger* and to Gide's *acte gratuit* as carried out by Lafcadio in *Lafcadio's Adventures*. The prosecutor understands the criminal only too well. He takes an attitude favorable to the accused, almost identifying with him. He understands how the cashier, previously conscientious, is driven to a desperate act by his need to escape from the treadmill after fourteen years of grinding monotony in his job. The prosecutor says: " 'There are moments when you are surprised at all those people who don't take up an ax. They all put up with life, although it is a phantom. Work as virtue. Virtue as a substitute for joy. And the other substitute, since virtue is not enough, is pleasure: holidays, weekends, adventures as experienced through the movies.' "

In the first nocturnal scene, the prosecutor instructs the housemaid to throw all his files into the fire, telling her that he had received a summons from Count Öderland, a legendary figure whose gruesome deeds were reflected and sung in folksongs all over the country. When the red reflections from the fire fill the whole room, the maid is reminded of "the charcoal burners in the woods when Count Öderland came." The prosecutor follows the summons and in the same night leaves his home and all his previous life.

In the third scene, when the prosecutor, assuming the identity of the legendary Count Öderland, has himself crowned by the charcoal burner's daughter (a merely symbolic act), the play becomes an obviously

contrived fantasy. He uses his newly acquired inner freedom to become a murderer himself—he kills three gen-
darmes and assembles around him a band of rebels
whose emblem is a black ax worn on the underside of
their jacket lapels.

Again, we are tempted to see a vague parallel to the
secret beginnings of the Nazi reign of terror in Germany. But it becomes clear from the subsequent scenes
that what Frisch is presenting has no relationship to actual historical events. Instead, he wants to imply an
existential condition basic to any person born in the
middle of the twentieth century. Count Öderland says:

"Where could you get nowadays without an ax? In this
world of papers, in this jungle of limitations and laws, in
this madhouse of order? . . . Leisure doesn't grow on trees
for us, or anything happy, unafraid, free, the beginning of
all that is called human. Nothing is a gift, everything is
earned. And everything is duty. Victory over oneself is the
greatest thing anyone can imagine, victory over oneself and
renunciation. It is a matter of conscience to stay alive. . . .
When dusk comes again, when all becomes gray, when
everything is shapeless, unreal, and the ghosts of responsibility arise, your conscience mushrooms until you suffocate
—or erupt."

After an unsuccessful attempt to retreat to the is-
land of Santorini (again, the actual place has only symbolic significance), Öderland and his band of rebels
operate as an underground movement, living in the cav-
ernous sewer installations of the city. Öderland becomes
more powerful and influential in the state, i.e., in a
world that does not know where it is going. Finally, he
is entrusted by the aging president with forming a new

government. Thus, the weak democratic state falls victim to Öderland's subversive revolutionary minority.

Again, is it not natural to take this as an allusion to Hitler, when he was asked by the eighty-five-year-old president of the Weimar Republic (1919-33), Hindenburg, to become chancellor of the republic and form a government of his own? Or is the action of this morality play just a means for indicating the weaknesses of democracy? In Zurich, in 1951, the public reacted negatively, feeling that the plot was too political and too close to home.

Count Öderland, like Frisch's *The Chinese Wall*, to which it is closely related, is also pessimistic. This becomes clear in the last scene, after the end of the prosecutor's dream adventures. Now, back at the fireside of his own home, he says: "Life is a phantom, I am beginning to understand that. . . . Repetition, that's it; even though you butt your head against the wall, that is the curse, that is the restriction, and an ax is no help against it." It becomes evident at the end that Öderland's visions have deceived him, that his temporarily adopted concept of life was wrong because it would never be able to bring about wealth and happiness, neither for himself nor for his followers.

The character of Count Öderland, in the final analysis, is not convincingly developed in the play. The first change in his character begins in the forest when Öderland begins to murder. The second murder without real motive (murder even for gain, jealousy, or revenge might be understandable) seems to be contrived. The constantly shifting scenes and the many subsidiary characters and side events dragged into the action confuse and strongly overshadow the theme of a man who becomes a criminal out of a belief that a man should have a higher life than that which is possible in everyday life, making the intent of the play hard to grasp. Frisch himself seems to have sensed this vagueness because at the end, he has the president say didactically, "Anyone who overthrows power in order to be free is taking over the opposite of freedom: power"—an aphorism that is not sufficiently realized throughout the twelve scenes. The spectator doubts the reality of the world from which the prosecuting attorney returns, disbelieving that Öderland ever really existed.

Within a period of five years Frisch wrote five major plays. Such productivity is not always to the best interests of the literary works. This is true of the fifth play, *Count Öderland*. Frisch, overwhelmed by the multitude of happenings in a world that was shattered but slowly rebuilding itself, scooped up his themes from it with both hands. Then, for him, the subject of European problems seems to have been written out for the time being. It was therefore fortunate that, in 1951, he received a fellowship from the Rockefeller Foundation for a year's study in the United States. This not only meant a broadening of his horizons and a personal renewal, but it also opened up an important new dimension in all his future work.

3

Dialogue and Monologue

*To write means
to read oneself*—M.F.

Before we follow Frisch into this new period of his expanding life, we should perhaps pause here to discuss his *Diary 1946–1949*, released in its final version in 1950. It is more than just an accompaniment to or commentary on his creative work, as is the case with many writers of our century, since the diary as an independent literary genre has come into its own. Not everything that such writers have set down can always be claimed to be of general interest. It is also more than the confessions somewhat typical of our age, which Thomas Mann once described as *sagesüchtig*, a word that expresses succinctly the meaning "afflicted by the urge to tell everything."

Frisch's diary is of quite a different sort. It is the product of an overabundance of experience and his surging reaction to it. Moreover, it expresses throughout the highest feeling of responsibility to his contemporaries inside and outside his own land and also—this interpretation does not seem exaggerated to me—to posterity. Of his diary it is inconceivable to say what Arno Schmidt once said about many diaries of present-day writers—that they are a "tail-wagging dance in front of a paper mirror." Instead, it comes much closer to a conception that Marie Luise Kaschnitz set down when she decided to keep a diary: that she hoped "to be able to live less complacently in it."

That Frisch published his observations of *only* the years from 1946 to 1949 is proof of how much responsibility Frisch felt toward his contemporaries who had to reconstruct the postwar world. Extensive traveling in the devastated countries of central Europe during the years following the holocaust of World War II is the most dominating aspect of these years of Frisch's life. That he preferred to travel and explore the miserable conditions in Germany, the country most horribly ravaged by the war, proves again how much he is able to sympathize with the suffering of his fellow humans without regard to whether or not they had caused the misery by their own deficiencies and guilt. For him these years thus became a time of great productivity, the very years in which the abyss of the postwar chaos gaped most widely, years that should have forced on every European a sense of higher responsibility than ever. Even those who had been "spared," like Frisch himself, had a special moral obligation to do some fundamental thinking and rethinking.

In the chapter "Café de la Terrasse," Frisch commented on the nature of the *Diary* itself in words that seem to me important as an introduction:

About the meaning of a diary—we live on a moving belt and there is no hope that we can get away from our former selves or change for the better any moment of our lives. We are the Then, even if we reject it, no less than the Now. . . . By not being silent about it, but recording it, you confess your thoughts, which at best correspond to the moment and the place at which they were conceived. You do not count on the hope that the day after tomorrow you will be wiser. You are what you are. You hold out your pen, like the needle in a seismological station, and we do not really write, instead we are written. . . . We can only, by bearing witness to the zigzag of our former thoughts and by exposing them to view, learn to know our nature, its confusion or its secret unity, its inescapability, its truth, which we cannot express accurately, not from the point of a single moment.

The 1950 publication of the *Diary* is an enlarged version of notes that appeared in 1947 under the title *Diary with Marion*. "Marion" is to be understood as the alter ego of Frisch himself. Frisch took the name Marion from the religious puppet plays of the Middle Ages in which the Virgin Mary was often one of the characters. The name marionette, the diminutive form, was given all the puppets. In the early days of his drama writing, Frisch may have felt that he, like a puppeteer, was manipulating his characters from behind the stage. Marion represents the creative power of Frisch, a spirit being related to Bin, who possesses the ability to talk with objects and angels as well as with others of his kind. Marion is a personification of the romantic Frisch, reappearing in a form similar to that which appeared in his early works, an identity that Frisch was not to abandon and exchange for another until 1947, when his *Diary* becomes realistic. Marion leaves a narrow but gleaming trail through the *Diary* in the pages recording 1946 and 1947; he is Frisch's inner traveling companion, his confirmation of himself. What Marion wants he admits in a conversation with an angel:

When I sit on the shore in the evening, I would like just once to be able to walk on the water, on the mother-of-pearl clouds reflected in its depths; or I would like, if I am standing on a hill . . . to stretch out my arms, as you do in dreams, and glide down over the slopes, over the darkening tips of the fir trees, over farmyards and roofs, away over the churchyard, the locked places—not even to fly like a bird, who mounts upward and rises. Oh, I would be content if you would let me glide, angel, only for a while; then back into the imprisonment of our weight. . . . But all that, angel, is not to be a dream. It should be completely real, the unbelievable.

The tendency to synchronize the imaginary and the real, at least for a moment, recurs constantly in Frisch's writings until 1950. Later these fleeting manifestations of his other self were strengthened psychologically and embodied in the characters of his plays as his artistic skill impressively grew. Thus he achieved density in his creations.

In the three-year diary as a whole, however, reality takes up much more space. Especially important are the travel accounts, one of the book's most extensive sections, which enables us to accompany Frisch back and forth through Europe, still bleeding from all its wounds in the early postwar years. In the course of these travels, we see that Frisch is always concerned with being objective, especially when he is observing conditions in Germany, though he reveals a genuine but not sentimental compassion for the very poor. One hesitates to attribute this to Frisch's Christianity, since his Christianity is incorporated in his work and hardly ever appears directly, i.e., without artistic disguise. But at the same time Christianity is a part of his native tradition, and who would deny that Frisch, as a genuine Swiss, is deeply rooted in that Christianity, a pietistic religion that discards the great, resounding word in favor of active aid to one's fellowman?

How easy it would have been, in his first encounter

with Germany in 1946, for Frisch to adopt a censuring tone, to make the point that the Germans had completely abandoned their moral standards, that they had been intoxicated by hybris and thus had brought upon themselves a terrible fate. Surely he knew that the inexorable law of cause and effect was at work here, but it would have been contrary to his innermost being to beat those who were already down. Frisch also knew that it was dubious that a writer could picture the misery that he found here with the means at a writer's disposal.

His travel pictures are memorable and vivid and could serve as timeless documents of Europe in ruins after 1945.

When you stand in Frankfurt, especially in the inner city, and when you think back on Munich . . . you can visualize what Munich was like, but not Frankfurt. A tablet indicates where the Goethe House stood. That you no longer walk on the old pavement increases the impression that the ruins are not standing, but sinking into their debris. I am often reminded of the mountains at home . . . narrow goat paths lead over the hills of rubble, and what is left standing seems to be the bizarre towers of a weathered mountain ridge. . . . At the station: refugees lie on all the steps, and you have the impression that they would not look up, even if a miracle took place in the center of the square, so certain are they that none could happen. . . . Their lives are unreal, awaiting without expectation, they are no longer attached to them; only life is attached to them, ghostlike, an invisible animal that is hungry and drags them through bombed stations, day and night, sun and rain; it breathes out of the sleeping children who lie on the rubble, their heads between bony arms, doubled up like embryos in the womb, as if they wanted to return there.

From 1946 to 1949 Frisch traveled almost entirely in Germany and its bordering countries. He stayed a number of times, and with special pleasure, in Berlin, a city divided into four parts and occupied by four nations, where the changed state of the postwar world could be seen more vividly, as though in a small and particularly clear mirror. On the occasion of his second trip to Germany, he describes his approach to Berlin in November 1947:

Entrance in the dusk of morning. The Havel Lakes, the sun rising behind trunks of pine trees, clouds, the bridges kneeling in the water, and the sun mirrored in it like brass. The roofs are wet. Between the tree trunks, a tangled mess of bullet-riddled searchlights. Then the first red flags . . . Morning on Alexander Square. The young rowdies and prostitutes. Much barter is going on—a three-penny opera without songs. Behind everything you sense a secret language. The uncanny thing is not that someone could attack you, at least not by day, but the knowledge that people like us, suddenly dropped into this life, would perish in three days. Occasionally you find a naked corpse, and the murderers naturally come from the other side. Whole districts are without a single light. It is impossible to estimate the enormous amount of rubble; and you simply turn your back on the question of what will ever become of it. A hilly landscape of bricks, with rubbish beneath and the stars shining above. The last thing to stir is the rats. In the evening a performance of Goethe's *Iphigenie*. . . . What do you say to Berlin? A foreigner's words of praise are rated highly; the need for recognition is gigantic. Anyone who assures the people now that Berlin's intellectual life is still unbroken is a great mind.

But on Frisch's next visit to Berlin in April 1948, he no longer merely recorded snapshots of the "moon landscape," the dispossessed and shattered life; he began to understand and evaluate what he had observed:

Evenings in company. The Berlin manner, which we at home are so likely to laugh at, I like very much—above all, the lack of sentimentality; the wit, consisting mainly of once again calling things what they really are; the anti-pathos, especially good to find in the German world. Here soulfulness is not spread like jam on the bread, wit is the chastest expression of emotion. Insouciance without rancor, sobriety—in times like these, the Berliners are admirable— that is, unchanged: unsentimental, concrete, active. . . .

Thoughts of Vienna, also divided into four zones of occupation like Berlin (which he admired more), oc-curred to Frisch:

Aber geh! In Vienna that is the magic formula that ban-ishes everything unpleasant. *Aber geh!* There the deluge is held back, runs off, simply evaporates from so much warmth of feeling. Vienna is still Vienna. No matter how bad things may be elsewhere, what does it matter to them? . . . In Berlin I feel more at ease.

From his first visits there, Berlin has held a special charm for Frisch to the extent that in the mid-1960s a newspaper item said that Frisch, who had been living in Rome since 1960, was considering for a while taking up residence again in the German-speaking world, and that this time he would feel inclined toward Berlin as his choice.

But Frisch's diary of that time is a valuable historical and human document not merely because of its account of his travels, but also because of his description of his encounters with people and the stimulation gained from them. Two writers in particular had a strong influence on him and his later works, as he himself has stressed: Albin Zollinger and Bertolt Brecht.

As of now Zollinger remains almost unknown to the general public in Germany. Nevertheless, in Switzerland he is recognized as having made a significant contribution to literature. He was preponderantly a poet, even in his prose, for which he won recognition. His novel *The Great Unrest* was especially well thought of. He was independent, argumentative, patriotic in the self-disparaging way of the Swiss (as Frisch also is), more active in thought than in deed, full of inner depths in contrast to his rather inconspicuous exterior ("His clothes as a whole reminded one of those of a village schoolteacher," writes Frisch in his commemorating paragraphs about Zollinger in the *Diary*). Frisch considered him, like Gottfried Keller, one of his spiritual family.

In the *Diary 1946–1949* Frisch devoted two beautiful, moving pages to his only meeting with Zollinger, which occurred in 1941 shortly before Zollinger died at the age of forty-seven of a heart attack.

Never will I walk across the Pfannenstiel without thinking, briefly or at length, about the writer I love most of all my modern countrymen—Albin Zollinger, who portrayed this landscape for all time. It was autumn, six years ago. I had just read his most recent book, and Constanze had to listen to a great deal of talk about it as we walked along this path together for the first time. I took her into a small inn that I knew from previous walks. There is a small walnut table there, in a window nook, where you can sit together and chat and look out at a splendid view. . . . Great was our disap-

pointment when we entered the place. The small table was
already occupied by a couple, and of course I was convinced
that we deserved the table more than they. Then, as the
man tilted his glass for the last sip, I suddenly heard myself saying, "Excuse me—but aren't you Albin Zollinger?"

"Yes," he said. "Why?"

I said I had just read his latest book. His expression
was noncommittal. He did not appear encouraging. . . . I
was distressed to realize that I, a younger man with nothing
to offer, had approached a mature, distinguished writer.
. . . What saved the moment was his touching pleasure as
we began to talk; he looked like a boy who for the first time
hears unqualified praise, or at least he appeared happy that
I was not crudely misinterpreting his work. Then he spoke
about Thomas Mann, whom he described as a master of
accuracy, about the limits of verbal expression, about how
frightening it was that any attempt to communicate can
succeed only by the grace of the sympathetic attitude of
others. He did not complain about the lack of it, but he
longed for once in his life, as he said, to write a page that
no one could misinterpret.

Zollinger can be called a regional writer, so long as
one leaves out the sentimental and bourgeois connota-
tions of the word. He was, almost against his will, a poet
of the mystique of nature, which he compellingly presented. He was especially involved in the landscape
around Lake of Zurich, which was always dominant in his
novels. Frisch's frequent, intense abandon, particularly
in his early works, to the moods of landscape showed his
absorption in nature, as he had discovered and learned
to love it, primarily through Zollinger's writings. Frisch's
description of the only meeting of the two writers, that
in the country inn on the Pfannenstiel (the famous

chain of hills above Lake of Zurich), has the masculine, tart tone that gradually was to mellow in Frisch's later writing but never to be totally relinquished. Landscape description, however, is still an important part of even his recent writing and is not the least of his excellences. Frisch, it is true, has never written poetry as such, but the lyrical element is a distinctive component of his prose.

The meeting with Bertolt Brecht took place in 1948. Frisch's great personal fascination with Brecht can be best understood by realizing the opposite natures of the two men. It speaks well for Frisch's intellectual strength and independence that his friendship with Brecht, as powerfully and lastingly as it enriched him, did not lead him away from himself and never led him to assume the role of a docile disciple.

Brecht, the older by thirteen years, had undergone many hard experiences, each of which had been not only fully lived through but also fully thought through. His achievements as a thinker were governed by a very definite discipline, that of the Marxist dialectic, and he would invariably be puzzled, actually exasperated, if someone he was talking to did not go along with him. At the same time, Brecht sought out opposition and was disappointed if he could not arouse it, for he was most in his element when waging intellectual warfare. Sometimes though, almost resisting, wrestling with himself, he retired into silent contemplation. The romanticism that was inherent in his nature was again and again suppressed by him, so that it would not hinder his service to the here and now—Frisch once spoke of him as a

"Jesuit of the Diesseits" (the here and now). The striving to change social conditions lay at the base of all his creative work. He tried to subordinate everything else to it, though he was too much of a poet to succeed invariably in this attempt.

Ten years after his death the whole world began to recognize Brecht's absolute greatness. The quarrel over his political philosophy has gradually retreated before his humane ethos, the deepest layer of his enormous lifework. Today Brecht is a part of world literature. Frisch realized very clearly the extraordinary proportions of this man's genius as early as 1948 when Brecht, then frequently characterized and branded as a "propagandist," was more caught in the crossfire of recognition and rejection than he is today. In this case death clarified, rather than transfigured, the man, and the distance of a decade has made possible a fairer judgement of his place in literature.

Frisch immediately recognized the chasm that lay between himself and Brecht; but he encountered Brecht's "superiority" modestly. "Brecht seeks completely abstract conversation. For my part, when Brecht checkmates with his dialectic, I have the least pleasure from our conversation; one is knocked out, but not convinced."

What differentiates Frisch fundamentally from Brecht is the absence in his plays of a strict methodology such as Brecht tried to maintain both toward ideology and style of presentation. In the main Frisch writes organically and Brecht according to a system. The "scientific" element in Brecht's drama, which he seemed to consider its real justification, is nowhere to be found in Frisch's work. At this time, Frisch's writings contain no exhaustive theoretical analysis of the art of the theater that might indicate that the plays were structured on theory rather than coming to life organically. A consciously formulated didactic element is completely absent from the theater of Max Frisch. He has, it is true, written detailed suggestions for staging many of his plays, notes about the genesis of an individual play, afterthoughts about it. This is particularly true of *Don Juan* and *Andorra*, for which he provided far-reaching elucidations and commentaries. Still, all such reflections and explanations are more spontaneous with him than with Brecht. Springing from his attitudes at the moment as they do, they do not adhere to any system or doctrine. Nonetheless, Frisch has the greatest respect for Brecht's fully conscious didactic tendencies and the origin of these tendencies, and it may even have been this orientation of Brecht's that led Frisch to think of him as a writer "superior" to himself.

In 1948, before returning to East Germany, Brecht lived for a time in an old gardener's cottage in Herrliberg on the Lake of Zurich. During these months he frequently sought Frisch's company, not only as a writer but also as an architect, since he saw architectural principles as being closely allied to his own writing principles insofar as the works produced both resulted from calculated planning. Brecht visited the building site of the Letzigraben swimming pavilion with lively interest and pleasure and wanted everything to be thoroughly shown and explained. In the *Diary* Frisch remarks on this:

With Brecht to the construction site. Since he never an-
swers the telephone during working hours, I had to fetch
him from his desk, as he wished me to do. As always when
he expects concrete information, he is ready to go immediately. . . . Of all the people I have escorted through the
project Letzigraben up to now, Brecht is by far the most
gratifying, eager to know, asking intelligent questions. Spe-
cialists easily forget the large, basic questions; laymen listen
and find solutions where a question was never raised. I find
the intellectuals especially thankless; before they have time
to understand something factual, they flee from it into
meditation, or a change of mood, sentimentalists, gasbags
of their wit or their subjectivity. Brecht has amazing vision,
an intelligence that attracts problems like a magnet, so that
they appear from behind the existing solutions. . . .

During this period Frisch read a number of Brecht's
theoretical writings, among which was *Five Difficulties
in Writing the Truth*. Brecht's most striking and famous
work of this kind, it has been called as important for our
century as Lessing's *Hamburgische Dramaturgie* was for
the eighteenth century. We read in Frisch's *Diary*:

The manuscript he gave me to read was called "Small
Organon for the Theater." Brecht wants to know what I
think. He considers even our misunderstandings useful;
they caution him. I have never before met a man who,
without affectation, is so free from self-importance. An
actor, not a great one, once dared to suggest a change in
the text—he wanted to say something where the script
called for him to be silent. Brecht listened to him, considered the matter, and agreed: not for the sake of yielding
but because what the man had said was right. His rehearsals
never have the air of a boudoir, but that of a workshop. In
other ways, too, Brecht has this serious readiness to learn,
which is not flattery and does not allow flattery, the imper-

sonal modesty of a wise man who learns from everyone who crosses his path—learns not from him, but through him.

The passage quoted above shows how strong an impression Brecht made on Frisch. More direct influences of Brecht's theories of the theater appear in some of Frisch's plays. But, thanks to Frisch's intellectual independence, there was never any possibility of direct borrowing or even of indirect imitation.

We are indebted to Frisch for his notes on Brecht, since they give us a deep insight into the life and creative art of one of the greatest literary figures of our century. At the same time, these same notes shed light on the nature and accomplishments of Frisch himself. A dialogue with "the other" involuntarily becomes a dialogue with oneself, too. Thus the relationship stimulated Frisch to recognize more clearly his own position and problems. All of Frisch's work takes its place midway between an emphatic political-social commitment in the Brechtian sense and an "art for art's sake" point of view. Frisch is indifferent to what is today called "the culture business." Even the word "culture" strikes him as suspect and undesirable. He avoids using it because it has become blurred and even soiled through increasing commercialization, and he prefers to replace the concept with the "clean," separate components that are believed to make up the collective term: music, literature, painting, architecture. Frisch is of the opinion that culture is far more than the total of the great symphonies that are composed in a certain nation. He thinks that many nations, and among them the Germans most dangerously, slightly distort the idea of culture in tying it too exclusively to the production of works of art. For Frisch, however, as a Swiss—and here he feels he is a true spokesman of his nation—culture means first of all civic virtues as they are proved by citizens of a nation in their respect and helpfulness for one another in daily life.

Frisch is committed, but he does not want to turn the work of art into a political tool. He preserves his personal dream beyond the level of politics and sees the political as only one aspect among many of a work of art. He believes a literary work can offer guidelines, incentives, direction to politics but not that the work itself should espouse a particular form of political activism. What the Italian writer Elio Vittorini once said in his *Open Diary 1929–1959* applies also to Frisch: that "the service the writer offers the human community is of such a delicate and involved kind that, at least at first glance, it may appear as an antisocial act." Although Frisch's work never goes so far that the word "antisocial" could be leveled against it, I quote this comment because it seems to me that it describes well how secondary direct "practical effect" is in Frisch's conception of a work of art.

Meanwhile, Frisch does not completely bypass political ideas. For, as he says in the *Diary*: "Anyone who is not concerned about politics has already acquired the political partisanship he wishes to avoid: he serves the ruling party." This is a typical statement of Frisch's and once again reveals directly how his mind takes the middle road and thereby makes it possible for him to be a fairer judge of his times. Perhaps it would be valuable for us to recognize him as an appraising voice of our era —and to listen. Can a member of one of the peoples not directly involved in the catastrophic political movements of our century achieve a penetrating and disinterestedly fair statement? Frisch's *Diary* seems to me to give a clear answer to this question, as does his succeeding work, which is increasingly earning a place in world literature.

4

The Other World

*The absurdity of our longing
to be different from what we are*—M.F.

I n 1945 Frisch used the quotation above to introduce a selection of photographs of scenes in various countries in an issue of the Swiss periodical *Atlantis*. The world beyond his own country and his exploration of it are an inseparable part of the man and the writer. Travel and meeting people of other origins and traditions are among his great passions, a fact to which we owe the wealth of landscapes and variety of characters in his work. In addition to his early travels as a journalist, Frisch traveled in Germany, Austria, and Italy between 1945 and 1951. He also visited Poland to cover the International Peace Congress, and France and Spain. From this active life he gained material for work after work. But even though his writing reflects the extraordinary breadth of his interest in the world, it never completely loses Switzerland as its starting point and center of gravity. He has extended his nationalism into a supranational humanity, without, however, slipping into wishy-washy internationalism. Frisch's writing during the 1950s, then, expands from the European terrain out into intercontinental.

Frisch's stay in America is reflected not only in "Our Arrogance toward America" (published in *Schweizer Rundschau*, 1952/53), an essay concerned with lessening anti-American bias, but also in the novels that followed it. Frisch's primary interest does not lie so much in the political or economic structure, and even less in the ethnology or geography of America, though we do find throughout "Our Arrogance toward America" magnificent descriptions of the landscape and customs. It lies rather in the social and human elements that he, as

a writer, experiences and contemplates in a world that is
new to him, relating and comparing them to the one he
already knows.

During his stay in America, Frisch lived for a while
in California, taking a trip into Mexico from there. In
1952 he stayed for six months in New York, the city that
is the quintessence of the image of the New World for
many Europeans who have never seen America. Frisch
tried to counteract this widely accepted view by calling
the West the "real America."

In general Frisch enjoyed life in the United States,
and he still cherishes the impressions and experiences
gained there. But essentially his feelings, as expressed
by Sybille in *I'm Not Stiller*, are that life in America,
though very pleasant, is not to his enthusiastic liking.
As far as interpersonal relationships are concerned,
Frisch found in America a greater distance between one
individual and another, between the "I" and the
"Thou," a greater withdrawal from social contacts into
mere civility, actually into smiling noncommittalism.
The following words of Sybille again express Frisch's
judgment on this point:

"Everything was agreeable, very pleasant as far as it went;
but a tension was lacking, a fullness of pregnant nuances,
a magic, a threat, the exciting possibility of a live entanglement. It was shallow, not unintellectual, for heaven's sake—
there were crowds of clever people, of educated people; but
it was lifeless, somehow without charm, without expectation. Life itself, the everyday things—shopping, lunch in the
drugstore, riding on the bus, waiting at the station, the this
and that which make up nine-tenths of our existence—it was
so unbelievably practical, so unbelievably dull. After twenty

minutes with these people you have got as far as you will
get after a year, and many more years will add nothing. The
relationship stays at the level of wishing one another well.
They make friends in order to have things pleasant, socially
or in some other way. And for the rest, there are psychia-
trists, like garage repairmen for the inner life, to go to when
you have a defect and can't repair it yourself."

Frisch does believe, however, that the spaciousness
of the country has imbued Americans with a different
dimension of thinking, an important impression for
Frisch, who would have liked to transplant a large part
of its wider horizons to Europeans. He particularly saw
in individual Americans a positive element of cosmo-
politanism, and from this he understood America's
greater readiness to help and its general openness to the
needs of mankind.

This is not the place to explore the accuracy of these
impressions of the American and his relations to the
world around him. What matters here is rather that it
helped Frisch to know better his own place in the world.
For the first time he became truly conscious of his own
relation to Switzerland—of himself in relation to and,
to a certain extent, in contrast to "idyllic Switzerland."
Among other realizations was the insight that the Swiss
in general do not dare to feel self-doubt. America came
to represent to Frisch the meeting with the world
abroad that helped to increase his sense of identity.
Repeated visits in subsequent years strengthened this
experience.

Written partly in New York and partly in Zurich,
the comedy *Don Juan, or The Love of Geometry* was

first produced in Zurich and Berlin simultaneously on 5 May 1953. This play also was subjected to several revisions. The final version appeared in 1962.

This play forms an important link in the long series of versions of the apparently immortal theme of Don Juan—from Tirso de Molina through Molière, da Ponte, Grabbe, Byron, and Shaw, to the present. For Frisch, Don Juan is a human prototype such as Icarus or Faust. But he gives a new interpretation to the traditional characterization of Don Juan and to his insatiable desire to seduce women. Frisch presents Don Juan as a narcissist and a woman hater who does not want to enter into a binding relationship with any woman because it would keep him away from his true passion: geometry. For him, each woman is only an episode. No encounter is different from another one. He deserts one after another because he loves something else more, something diametrically opposite to the fickle and incomprehensible psyche of the female: geometry, a science of precise laws, the apprehension of which offers the masculine spirit an aspiration more worthy than love.

In the five acts of his Don Juan comedy Frisch shows us Don Juan as a developing person rather than the Don Juan who begins and ends as an accomplished lover and seducer of women, which had been the traditional way of presenting him. The first act takes place the night before Don Juan is to be married to Donna Anna, the daughter of Sevilla's Grand Commandant. Don Juan tries in vain to flee because he begins to feel that marriage would become an imprisonment for him. In the second act, when Don Juan and Donna Anna

stand in front of the altar, Don Juan flatly says "No."
And when Donna Anna's father challenges him to a
duel, Don Juan refuses this, too. The following night he
takes refuge with his friend Rodrigo's bride, in whose
house the insulted and enraged Rodrigo finally discovers
him. A free-for-all takes place, which results in the
deaths of Don Juan's father (a commandant), Don
Rodrigo, and Donna Anna.

In the fourth act we see Don Juan himself prepare
and stage a "descent to hell" in order to escape the fate
of being trapped in marriage by Miranda, a former pros-
titute, now the widow of the Duke of Ronda. For the
ceremony, Don Juan invites the Bishop of Cordoba, too.
" 'No hell without the church,' " says Don Juan. Don
Juan tells the bishop that now he wants to leave the
world, dissatisfied as he is by the two sexes into which
the world is divided. He suggests that in actuality he be
admitted to a monastery cell in order to finally escape
his moral reputation and the bad example it has for the
rising generation. The bishop, however, is not a real
clergyman but Balthasar Lopez, the husband of one of
Don Juan's lady friends. Now the staging of his "descent
to hell" has its start without encumbrance, whereby the
act ends.

The fifth act, then, shows that such a way out can
never be real, only imaginary. Just as Count Öderland
was unable in the end to change his fate by associating
with criminals, so is Don Juan unable to escape his pre-
determined fate: the union in marriage with a woman,
Miranda.

In Frisch's interpretation, Don Juan, in his innermost life, remains truly without a thou. He can no more find a thou among men than among women, for his libido is cathected only with his own ego. Thus he can be unashamed in seeking his egocentric self-fulfillment. But he is not entirely shameless, since his lust is only a role played to hide his true nature from the world, to the point of disavowing his real self. The traditional Don Juan presents the image of a man without any real attachments, and it is not merely by chance that he was always portrayed as remaining childless. His comedian's mask was always the other side of a secret tragedy, the tragedy of being a barren hybrid. But Frisch hesitates to call him a nihilist, which he considers a much abused catchword; as he wrote in his *Diary*, and again in the *Afterthoughts to Don Juan*, it is a word "that at times can cause the greatest harm. Within a society of general untruthfulness, everyone is called a nihilist who wants to find out what is true." Frisch sees in Don Juan, as a type, the Spaniard whose masculine image, so strongly determined by the bullfighter, must be confirmed in activities that correspond to Don Juan's encounters with women: "The black animal that Don Juan faces up to is the innate power of sex, which he, in contrast to the bullfighter, cannot kill without killing himself," Frisch writes in the *Afterthoughts to Don Juan*.

Frisch does not permit Don Juan, as a great sinner, to fall victim to the tortures of hell. Instead, he is cunningly entangled in the nets of Miranda, who is expecting his child, and even calmly submits to being married to her.

It is an uncommonly clever, wittily pointed play,

which offers a broad view of the relativity of all human
sentiment. It glitters throughout with irony and parody.
Love, stripped of its absolute power, is only a romantically playful pastime of the hero, who, in the words of
the theater critic Siegfried Melchinger, is "unmasked as
a frustrated geometrist mistreated by women." Frisch
confesses in his *Afterthoughts to Don Juan* that it was
specifically the poetic possibilities that tempted him to
undertake a new version of the subject matter—including a complete reversal of the legend—or, quite simply,
"the desire to write a piece for the theater."

A "henpecked Don Juan" is Frisch's last trump in
the play. "The extraordinary tends to reach the point
where it looks dreadfully similar to the ordinary." It is
an ingenious work from the first conception of the idea
on, and the main theme is developed faultlessly to a
convincing ending. One cannot but agree with Friedrich Luft, an outstanding German theater critic, who,
after its premiere, called *Don Juan* Frisch's very best
play, well-rounded in form and content.

Does Frisch's own unsuccessful experience with his
first marriage lie behind the play? Is it Frisch's own
despair that is reflected in Don Juan's words when he
says that every man has something he regards more
highly than women after he has sobered up, and that he
feels happy when the love affair, like a stifling storm, is
over? This Don Juan, who is "loved out," who experiences love affairs in a purely functional way, who lets
love happen to him—bored, almost against his will—instead of bringing it about as an expression of his will, is
the reverse of the archetypal Don Juan as he appears in

other literary treatments where mask and essence are not so widely separated. The twentieth-century man, inclined to rationalism, can more readily recognize himself in Frisch's Don Juan than in the characterizations of Don Juan of past centuries. The gallantry of Frisch's Don Juan, playful and cynical, is a camouflage for his actual inability to love. Here Don Juan denies the absolute values of love as attributed to it in the literary works of the Western tradition, where human emotions of elective affinity toward another human being are most cherished and held most sacred.

The play offers its audience or readers the greatest pleasure. But at the same time it succeeds in giving more meaningful insight into the depths of the world of emotions, into the typical emotional life of present-day man, who prefers observing his feelings to abandoning himself to them.

It is with the pleasure of listening to a good modern storyteller that we read Frisch's novel *I'm Not Stiller*, written in 1953 and published in 1954. Yet, the charm of the engrossing story should not blind one to its deeper layers. It is an extraordinary book in every way, one that has now raised Frisch to the first rank of novelists in the German language. Although *The Difficult Ones* was a good and pleasant work, it was a traditional novel, a work of the level of literary excellence achieved by many other gifted writers. But *I'm Not Stiller* is a completely original work in which the author found his very own individual form. In a time that "has styles, but no style," as the German literary critic Walter Jens said, in the literary landscape of our age—which is more amorphous than contoured—it stands as a point of direction, i.e. a new technique of novel writing can be learned from it.

The fate of Stiller is that of a man who has grown alien to himself and who wants to become another in order to be able to "accept himself"—a leitmotiv that we will now begin to encounter frequently in Frisch's works. The story begins when a man, an artist, who is crossing the Swiss border in a passenger train, is confronted by a representative of the state: the conductor who checks the passengers' passports. The passenger Stiller, who is returning after an absence of six years to his native country—the reason for his return is not expressly given—obstinately insists on being the Mr. White of the American passport he holds. But one of the fellow passengers had read an article in an illustrated magazine about Stiller, a famous Zurich sculptor who, when suspected of being a Soviet spy, fled the country. He notices the overpowering resemblance of this man who calls himself Mr. White, to Stiller. Stiller is arrested and put on trial.

"I'm not Stiller! Day after day I say it, I swear to it. . . ." These words that begin the novel plunge into the middle of its theme. The sequence, flowing back and forth through events of the past and the present, is executed so perfectly from beginning to end that the time levels, continually shifting and interwoven as they are in the human psyche, at last reveal the truth. In prison the alleged Mr. White begins to make notes on the past life of the missing Stiller. Stiller had in fact run away from himself out of dissatisfaction, conscious

of his misspent life, of having been a failure in wartime
(as a soldier in the Spanish Civil War), of having failed
at marriage with the tender, beautiful, but somewhat
frigid dancer Julika. The marriage had dissolved into
indifference and ended with Stiller's flight into a love
affair with Sybille, the wife of the man who is now the
prosecuting attorney. The affair, however, did not lead
to inner release for the two, since Stiller repeatedly saw
Julika reflected in Sybille and could not completely free
himself from this. Stiller remained alienated in all his
human contacts, and wavered back and forth between
reality and his fantasy of abandoning his Stiller persona.

During Mr. White's trial, he is confronted with all
the people of Stiller's previous life and is caught more
and more tightly in the net of Stiller's inescapable past.
Finally, the sight of Stiller's former sculptures forces
him, as it were, to a decision. Mr. White destroys everything that is a tangible witness to Stiller's past, for he
considers that past dull, good for nothing, and does not
want to be identified with it. But people have formed
an image of him—Frisch's recurring leitmotiv—and he
himself is only wearing a mask that he believes makes
him unrecognizable. Unknown to himself, however, he
also made an image of the people who were part of his
life in the past, and he has oppressed himself with these
images. Since the making of unalterable images can
never lead to clearness, let alone happiness (due to the
fact that every individual is subject to changes throughout his lifetime), Stiller lived restlessly during the years
of his voluntary exile. Yet he felt compelled to keep
these fixed images formed in his soul, no matter how far

he traveled in the world. The whole vicious circle can be broken only when Stiller learns to accept himself.

The court verdict helps him to do this. It clearly determines the identity of Stiller-White and assesses him with only the fines he has incurred by disappearing suddenly and neglecting his duties as a citizen. In the end Stiller recognizes the inevitability of the law, which, in this case, leads him back to the law of his own being. "I feel that I am unconditionally ready to be no one else but the man I have been from birth," Stiller notes at the end of his painful journey through self-alienation.

It does not seem accidental that when Stiller admits to being nobody else but Stiller, he stops reflecting about the possibilities of changing a personality by willfully changing name and way of life. He learns the hard way to accept himself with both his positive and negative characteristics and thus becomes more quiet within himself, though not happier. The law, which in the end proves to be his helper and friend, is secretly predisposed in his favor, specifically because the prosecuting attorney, from the beginning of the trial to the end, is the one who understands Stiller's "case" best and treats him most humanely. He says:

"I see Stiller not as a special case. I see in him several of my acquaintances, myself among them, even though they may offer different examples of how to demand too much of oneself. . . . Many know themselves, but few come to the point of accepting themselves. It requires the highest stamina to be able to accept oneself."

After the verdict is announced, Stiller and his former wife, Julika, retire to a secluded life in the country.

(Beneficent circumstances enable the prosecuting attorney and Sybille, as well as Stiller and Julika, to make new beginnings, after extensive detours and estrangements. The final acceptance of the identities and also of the marriages seems to be a form of purification suited to our times.) On a lonely farm, where Stiller begins to operate a small pottery, Julika falls ill with tuberculosis and dies in a nearby hospital. Stiller's former prosecutor, Sybille with him, stands by in the difficult night of his bereavement. With the words: "Stiller remained in Glion and lived alone," the story dies away—a life history deeply contemplated and vividly brought alive.

To deal thoroughly with all the rich facets of this work would require many pages. Quantitatively the novel's narrated action is small in proportion to Stiller-White's entries in his diary and his letters, which cover it like climbing ivy. There are not too many things happening in the course of the story unless we take self-introspection as a fascinating journey full of adventures —as has been the case ever since the 1920s, when psychoanalysis first entered fiction. In most cases the technique of a diary within a novel is used to show the underlying forces that motivate an individual's actions.

Chosen with masterly skill, Frisch's words in this novel give the effect of being casually noted down. While in prison, Stiller-White, in humble self-explanation, scrutinizes his bungled life, and by giving an account of it begins to find sense in it. The double existence achieves a wonderfully convincing unity in his notes. We can almost think of *I'm Not Stiller* as a picaresque novel, if we consider carefully the prosecuting attorney's statement in his afterword: "His love of pranks, like Till Eulenspiegel, never left Stiller. He needed a certain amount of disguise in order to feel at ease among people. Looking at him, I could not imagine how he endured his existence, how any man, once conscious of his real experiences and thus freed of all vain expectations, could endure existence." But this viewpoint is made untenable by the high degree of resignation that finally enters Stiller's life, with which we are able to sympathize, whereas the traditional picaro remains incomprehensible to us and inimitable.

Stiller's personality appears to us in the many configurations of the conscious and the unconscious, sometimes in the words of the "I" who tells his story, i.e., Stiller-White, and at other times in the meditations of the prosecuting attorney. The novel also offers many-sided views of questions of contemporary life, which make it a compendium of our times. The twofold charm of this literary work of art rests in the fact that it delves deeply into a man's interior while keeping the action rather narrowly circumscribed.

The success of *I'm Not Stiller* was extraordinary. This and Frisch's concurrent success as a playwright at a time when German-language drama was stagnating, when the only German drama writing of literary excellence was being done almost exclusively by himself and Friedrich Dürrenmatt, another outstanding Swiss writer, brought Frisch a number of prizes: the Wilhelm Raabe Prize of the city of Braunschweig in 1955, the Schiller Prize of the Swiss Schiller Foundation in 1955, and the Welti Prize for Drama of the city of Bern in 1956. By

1956, inspired by a second trip to the American continent that included Mexico and the Yucatan, Frisch was already working on a new novel that was to bring him even greater success: *Homo Faber*. This novel is, like *I'm Not Stiller*, the story of an ego. It is more typical of the spirit of the twentieth century than *I'm Not Stiller*.

Homo Faber, which is simply subtitled "A Report," is a brilliant interpretation of a human type that has become dominant in our century—the man whose confidence in life is based almost exclusively on his own efficiency, who shapes his own life along rational lines. But at the same time the novel contains a warning. Walter Faber, the protagonist, is an austere man of technology, governed by the laws of mathematics, who is structuring and leading his life according to scientific rules; a man who, repudiating any form of mysticism, perceives life itself only on a rational scale. He says: " 'I do not believe in destiny and fate; as a technician I am used to dealing with the formulas of probability. Why providence? I don't need any sort of mystique in order to accept improbability as a fact of experience. Mathematics is enough for me.' "

Refusing to recognize the imponderables of existence, Faber is bound to fail as a human being. Although Frisch nowhere expressly says it, his underlying appraisal of Faber is that the latter, by lacking any form of transcendental orientation, is in the end a poor and deplorable man. As a successful executive, as an electrical engineer of power plants on several continents, and in his work with an organization called Technical Help for

Underdeveloped Peoples, Faber is a homeless, constant
traveler, a passenger on many airlines. Traveling has
long since lost all its romance for him. Unforeseeable,
surprising events thrust themselves into his life again
and again. But he does not concede that they are anything more than that, that decisions are made for us
that come from a source far beyond our understanding.
He believes that events of all kinds are only the result of
scientific laws that will subsequently be revealed. In being insensitive to the miraculous phenomena of life, he
is dissociated from any real feelings of happiness and unhappiness. Everything that he does is an act of the will
and male energy, "nothing but sums." He has been re-
proached with living "as if there were no old age" because he has never been inclined to think farther than
the next day and his next commitment.

From the beginning on, an aura of tragedy hangs
over Faber's life, and Frisch, no doubt, wanted pur-
posely to give the reader this impression. From the very
first lines, the reader cannot escape the feeling that all
of Faber's experiences, even those that reveal him as the
sole master of his life, are traumatic. He cannot help
seeing Faber as a victim of self-misunderstanding and
false orientation to life, a victim of overevaluation of
material success. Serving and obeying only the claims of
the surface of things and of the present, Faber is continually being tripped up and overcome by his past and
the unrecognized world inside him. That is, being God's
creature, he, too, is subject to those experiences in life
that are beyond our human reasoning and that spring

from sources other than those we are able to identify and comprehend.

On a flight to Caracas, Faber meets a man with whom he has to spend four days and three nights when an engine failure forces delay in the Mexican desert of Tamaulipas. After many conversations, he recognizes his fellow passenger as the brother of his former best friend and fellow student, Joachim. Twenty years before Faber had lived in Zurich with Joachim, but the relationship had ended when Joachim married Faber's sweetheart, Hanna, who was pregnant with Faber's child. The child had grown up thinking Joachim was her father. Hanna and Joachim were later divorced, and the child had remained with her mother.

Later, on a voyage from New York to Europe, Faber meets a young girl "in black cowboy trousers," with reddish-blonde hair in a ponytail, who fascinates him. He begins a love affair with her and even proposes marriage, although he is a bachelor over fifty years old. " 'I thought of marriage as I never had before.' " He calls her Sabeth, a shortening of her first name, Elisabeth. He does not know that she is the daughter he and Hanna had begotten. Because of his passionate attachment to Sabeth, he accompanies her on a trip to Greece, where he and Hanna meet again. Separated from her second husband, a communist named Piper, whom she had married in the intervening years, Hanna is now working in an archeological institute in Greece. Their meeting leads to Faber's recognition of his entanglement in incestuous guilt. On an excursion Sabeth is bitten by a snake and falls in such a way that she suffers a skull fracture, which causes her death several days later. Faber decides to settle in Greece and remain with Hanna. He makes one more business trip to South America and, on his return to Athens, falls victim to cancer of the stomach and dies.

Greece, as the final setting in which the conflicts of this dramatic story are resolved, brings to the reader's mind the ancient dramas of guilt and atonement. The presentation, very different from *I'm Not Stiller,* and the rough, sometimes sophisticated and casual language give a disturbing effect to the course of events and the conversations, endowing the novel as a whole almost with the impact of a play. Toward the end Faber's restlessness, as death draws closer and closer, is magnificently characterized by phrases that become shorter, by thoughts often abandoned in midsentence.

As Faber begins to sense subconsciously the wrongness of his world view—to suspect gropingly that there is no life fully rewarding and satisfying without a strong belief in forces superior to ourselves—the wrongness of his arrogant solitude begins to dawn on him. How otherwise could he have made the decision to finally settle with Hanna after having led such a rugged and often disrupted life? The egocentric way of life he had chosen could not but make all his decisions arbitrary and in the end irresponsible—so much so that life itself provided the punishment when he fell in love with his own daughter. For a man who feels himself sole master of his life, completely independent of providence, let alone of mercy—a man for whom the word "mercy" practically does not exist—life is bound to end in unhappiness and despair. His modern form of Promethean arrogance, however, has to be expiated as all such forms of self-aggrandizement have to, although Faber never, even when dying, becomes conscious of the fact that we have to pay for everything we do wrong. We can gather this from the lines he sets up as sort of a testament:

"Arrangements in case of death: all evidences of my life, such as reports, letters, looseleaf notebooks, shall be destroyed; everything is wrong. To be in the world: to be in the light. Somewhere (like the old man recently in Corinth) to drive an ass, our profession—but above all: to stand firm in the light, the joy (as our child's, when she sang) of knowing that I will be extinguished in the light over heather, asphalt, and sea, standing firm in time, as it were, eternity in a moment. To be forever: to have been."

A man who faces death in such a way can be considered purified in the sense of ancient secular religiosity although the word "eternity" exists for him as little as does the word "mercy." His affirmation of light is not a disavowal of himself—as an end in mystic twilight would be—because this would leave open at least a vague possibility of being protected by superior forces beyond our human reasoning. Faber seeks consolation not in any sort of life beyond the grave but rather in the reflected splendor of the phenomena of life itself, to which he gave himself unreservedly, in all his active life and, most consequently, even in his death. Faber's seemingly shattered life is redeemed at its end by his experience of a secular, parareligious act of grace. This act, harmonious in itself, ends the life journey of a man who is typical to a great extent of the midtwentieth century.

In this joining of ancient and modern motives of fate, as well as in the union of epic and dramatic elements, the novelist and dramatist Frisch has, in *Homo Faber*, attained a power of expression that is nothing less than splendid. It makes the work, in my opinion, the high point of Frisch's work to date.

Homo Faber is the story of the practical man of action who, in spite of all his efficiency and rationalism, could not find happiness in life because he ignored and denied the role of superior forces in that which is called life. He was foreshadowed in Frisch's writing by the small businessman and hair-tonic manufacturer, Biedermann. Frisch first presented this character in a satire in 1948 (now included in his *Diary 1946–1949*), in a radio play called "The Firebugs" in 1953, and in a one-act play of the same title, published in 1958. With this distorted presentation of another but no less typical man of today, Frisch gets to the brink of the "theater of the absurd." He called the play a "lecture without a lesson," thus linking it to a dramatic genre that Brecht was committed to. But Frisch's form of the didactic play differs substantially from that of Brecht's. The comic element predominates. Where Brecht announces the "lesson" at the end, Frisch (in the manner of the theater of the absurd, which does not intend to teach a lesson) allows his reader only a glimpse of the abyss between good and evil. By doing this, he runs the danger, it is true, of having the whole thing taken as a big joke.

Biedermann is self-assured but, behind a false mask of humaneness, he is also egotistical and self-satisfied,

cowardly, and, like most members of the petite bourgeoisie, a follower of the majority. He believes that he
and his possessions are being threatened by the frightening, homeless "firebugs" who ply their criminal activities
in the city and who have taken up residence in his attic
for a few days. By means of false geniality and hospital-
ity, he believes he can make these men become his
friends. At the same time, he coldly dismisses an em-
ployee who has served him faithfully for many years,
thus driving him to suicide. Biedermann is stupid and
intellectually dependent, thus easy to deceive. His eager-
ness to be respected and popular makes him willing to
sign a compact with the devil himself, whom he refuses
to recognize as such. In the end, he and his wife, all his
possessions, and the entire town are destroyed by the
firebugs. A pseudo-Greek chorus of "fire fighters," ironically commenting on the whole affair in dactylic verse,
speaks the final words:

> "Much is senseless, and nothing
>   More senseless than this story:
>   Which, to be sure, kindles the flames
>   And kills many, alas, but not all
>   And changes nothing at all."

The conditions of our time that gave birth to this
play are clearly evident. But, on the other hand, they are
only an occasion for the creation of the play, which is
to be regarded as an allegory and not, for example, as a
key to "Michel" (the epithet for the stereotyped German) or to the 1948 overturn of the government in
Czechoslovakia, which has frequently been mentioned
in connection with this play. Instead of being a bur-

lesque (a play written for no other reason than to make
the audience laugh, with no ambition whatsoever of social criticism), *The Firebugs* is a general satire of the
times, told from the perspective of those who, unsus-
pectingly, do everything possible to become the victims
of their murderers. Biedermann is simply the representative of the gullible and easily led opportunist: his
point of view is the lack of a point of view. He wants to
be able to rest in the knowledge of his good deeds, as we
are taught in Sunday School; beyond that, he wants
"rest and peace, and that is all."

Biedermann is caught in the first trap set for him,
and he clasps "the vipers to his bosom." It is possible
to connect this to the mass of German citizens who, during the unemployment and confusion of the early 1930s,
were in such panic and need that they sold themselves
to Hitler without realizing what was involved. But
Frisch does not want the work to be given such an ob-
vious interpretation. He does not want to turn the stage
into a political arena, since, from his point of view,
politicizing drama is not art. Frisch regards his Biedermann more as a symbol of Everyman in the twentieth
century—that is, the mass man, who, no longer creative
himself, deals with and disposes of the creative contribu-
tions of others, the man who is a slave to business, the
authorities, and bureaucracies. His situation becomes
absurd only when the allegorical action ceases and the
empty, false routine of emotions takes over. It is that
"empty good-naturedness" that Martin Esslin mentions
in his excellent book on the theater of the absurd, in
which he says that, because of this good-naturedness,

"the destruction of values has reached a point where the bewildered individual can no longer decide which things to keep and which to destroy."

The Firebugs was first produced on 29 March 1958 in Zurich. Because of its shortness it was followed by a short farce, *The Great Rage of Philip Hotz*. In May of the same year it had its second premiere in Frankfurt. For this production Frisch wrote an "Afterpiece" that takes place in hell, where Biedermann claims for damages he suffered as a victim of arson. He and his wife are spared and allowed to return to earth by the lord of the underworld, who is no longer interested in punishing the minor sinners while the doers of capital crimes are pardoned by Heaven itself. At the end we see again the firebugs cycling into the newly built town to commit new crimes—and practically nothing has been changed. Like many others, Biedermann, who has been completely burned out and deprived of all his property, has really learned nothing from the catastrophe. The bleakness of the empty stage on which we see him at the very end of the play corresponds to the emptiness of his own mind. He thinks only of indemnification, for was he not always a good, law-abiding, well-meaning man? In the general rebuilding of his ruined city, he will soon know where to find a hearth on which to brew his bowl of soup again. Satirically the chorus sings to him (and to us):

"More splendid than ever
 Is our beautiful city
 Rising again from ruin and ashes,
 The rubble is completely swept away and forgotten.
 Also quite forgotten are those

> Who were burned to a crisp there
> And their screams from the flames—
> Dead history they have already become."

Once again, Frisch remains a pessimist.

In 1958, Frisch was honored several times: with the Charles Veillon Prize (Lausanne) for *Homo Faber*, with the Georg Büchner Prize (Darmstadt), and finally with the Literature Prize of his home city, Zurich, whose delay in recognizing his many works had long puzzled Frisch. His relationship, in general, to Switzerland is an ambivalent one, a mixture of defiance and love. Joachim Kaiser even speaks of Frisch's "raging anti-Swiss emotion," although this would seem to me to be an exaggeration. Plainly Frisch's speech in Zurich on the occasion of the presentation of the prize unmistakably shows his relationship to his homeland. He mentioned "our own Switzerland, our liberal country, which has so many rebellious writers," among whom he counted himself. But then he summed up his feelings for his native land in four short sentences, which have already attained a sort of fame and which are truly worth quoting here: "My environment, the one most closely surrounding me, is Switzerland. And for that I am grateful. But Switzerland is not my only environment. And for that, too, I am grateful." Who can read these lines without thinking of Goethe's statement: "I am an inhabitant of Weimar, I am a citizen of the world"?

After a third journey to America, in 1960, Frisch's next drama, *Andorra* (a play in twelve scenes) appeared. This play has often been interpreted as a "lecture with a lesson" in the sense of Bertolt Brecht. Yet

Frisch says that it is not to be read as such. Nor, he says, is it to be read as an allegory of the anti-Semitism of the Nazis. Frisch had been concerned with the theme of *Andorra* as early as 1946, but it was not until the fall of 1961 that it was presented.

Once again, we should no more identify the title *Andorra* with the tiny state in the Pyrenees than we should interpret Peking or Santa Cruz geographically in Frisch's earlier works. Andorra is used only as a symbol of the small state bordered by a large, imperialistic one, under whose constant threat it lives and suffers. Its citizens, who must always be wary, live in continual fear of siege and subjugation. Among them lives Andri, a youth who has barely outgrown adolescence, at once rough and gentle. The village thinks he is a Jew who was rescued from the large neighboring nation of the "Blacks" during a period of anti-Semitic persecution, and Andri himself believes this story. But in reality he is the illegitimate child of the village teacher and a Señora of the land of the Blacks, in which Andri was born. The teacher has raised the boy, along with his legitimate daughter, Barblin, to gain standing as a moral person but at the same time with understanding and love. Andri, unaware of his real parentage, falls in love with Barblin—a reappearance of the incest motif of *Homo Faber*. The teacher's reluctance to allow Andri to marry Barblin has only one meaning to Andri: that he is denied his beloved because he is a Jew, for a Jew is "not like them, not cheerful, not easy-going, not like them"— that is, not like the majority.

In Andri's beautiful and deeply touching conversation with the priest, there echoes the tragedy of one who, through no fault of his own, belongs to a minority that is always in the wrong. Andri is fully convinced that the teacher does not want to give him his daughter in marriage for no other reason than that he is a Jew, and he bitterly complains about it. In vain the priest tries to appease Andri's bitterness of heart and, moreover, warns him not to misinterpret everything adverse that happens to him in life as an expression of anti-Semitism. He accuses Andri of being oversensitive in this respect. But the unhappy boy has stiffened so much in his acquired method of defense that it seems to be impossible to help him.

The one who experiences *Andorra* from this point of view will, no doubt, get the deepest comprehension of the problem that the play presents. The transformation of the non-Jew into a Jew makes doubly clear the fate of ethnic minorities. Andri, forced into the role of Jew, no longer wants to give it up, not even when he is told that he is not a Jew. For, reacting to the people in his environment, he has in the meantime learned to accept himself as a Jew and is now determined to remain one. The lie is laid bare when the Señora comes to visit. Andri, her son, describes her as a "fantastic woman." He has "a kind of feeling" about her that she had once been the mistress of the teacher. Even when the truth about his parentage is revealed, Andri will not abandon the role that has been forced upon him:

"Since I was first able to hear, people have told me that I am different. And it is so, I am different. And I have also considered whether it's true that I think about money all the time; when the people of Andorra think that I am thinking about money, they are usually right: I do think of money all the time. And they have said to me that my kind is cowardly. I didn't want to admit it, what they said to me, but it is true. It is true what they say: I do not feel as they do. And I have no home. Your Reverence has said one must accept that, and I have accepted it. Now it is up to you, Your Reverence, to accept your Jew."

This scene expresses bitter irony. In Andri's words, Frisch reveals again the concept that has played such an important part in his previous works: that the image we build of a man affects that man and becomes fixed in his own mind; that such an image can bear any sort of features, and it makes no difference whether or not it corresponds to reality; and finally, that such images are death-giving. At the beginning of the eighth scene, the kneeling priest expresses this conclusion very clearly: " 'Thou shalt make unto thyself no graven image of God thy Lord, nor of men, who are his creatures. I, too, was guilty. I wanted to approach him [Andri] with love when I spoke with him. But I, too, made unto myself an image of him, I, too, fettered him, I, too, brought him to the stake.' "

When the Blacks do finally attack Andorra and occupy it, Andri is led away as a Jew. He does not resist death, but he does resist a soldier's attempt to take away the ring the Señora had given him. The last we hear from him, surrounded by Black soldiers, is a shriek when a soldier chops off his finger for the ring. His father, who was the cause of the whole fraudulent situation, hangs himself, while Barblin, her head shaved because of her unseemly love for a Jew (what the people

of Andorra consider a punishable, racial sex deviation),
distraught, returns to whitewash the houses of the village, carrying Andri's shoes in case he returns.

Should Andri's execution have been shown on the
stage? It was originally planned that way. But Kurt
Hirschfeld, the director of the first production, clearly
grasped Frisch's intentions and made him conscious of
them when he deleted the execution scene. Frisch understood that showing the execution, and thus ending
the play on a gruesome note, would weaken the impres-
siveness of the play. Even the stake was taken away, and
nothing but the troubled priest's words mentioning the
stake was left. Thus the stake became more convincingly what it had been intended to be from the beginning: a symbol.

In this work again, with special clarity, Frisch issued
a warning against prejudice, which, when carried to ex-
tremes, can lead to the murder of millions. Because it is
placed in a more comprehensive context, however, the
play should not be read as a strictly didactic tract
against anti-Semitism. Since the spectrum of the Jewish
experience was at hand, Frisch used it to show the fate
of a member of a minority, deprived of his rights, who
in the end wants nothing but the alienation and misery
that have been forced upon him. After the monstrous
crime perpetrated against the Jewish people in our century, a play such as this, a side product of the events,
can only serve as a beacon and a summons to a new
consciousness.

The play, dedicated to the Züricher Schauspielhaus,
was first produced there on 2 November 1961. It was pre-

sented in Munich, Frankfurt, Düsseldorf and Berlin a year later, and these productions helped to spread the play's influence rapidly and to give it the fame it deserves for its ideas and dramatic power. But its impact has, until now, remained limited to central Europe, where excesses such as those in the play were experienced first hand. Understandably, equally strong interest was lacking in London and in New York. Only the future will determine which facet of the work will predominate in the end: its relevance, as a factual play, bound to the historical moment, or its creative brilliance, independent of the times, for which the moment only provides the occasion. In Frisch's development as an artist, it marks an important step toward greater clarity and depth, by means of simplifying and sharpening the line of action and the language. It marks his development from a poet of the stage, strongly inspired by the romantic, into a dramatist who endeavors to enlighten.

In a speech to drama critics in Frankfurt's Church of Saint Paul in 1964, Frisch conceded in an indirect manner that he sees the function of the drama as that of enlightening. This attitude came through in his criticism of the theater of the absurd: "The public that is content with the absurd would delight a dictator: it does not want enlightenment about fundamentals; it wants only to enjoy what frightens." Since *The Firebugs* Frisch has undoubtedly thought of himself as a teacher. But he remains skeptical about the possibility of changing the world by means of works of art (here again, in contrast to his great contemporary, Brecht). In that speech he said that such a function could hardly be expected of a work of art. Frisch, however, believes that literature, even if it cannot change the world in which we live, can at least call it into question, and he sees a value in this. He doubts that literature could ever become the basis for the "inner direction" of man, and he says this with special emphasis, pointing out that German history, "taken all in all, has been very little influenced by the great literature of Germany from Schiller to Brecht." Frisch wants neither to overestimate nor to underestimate. He is constantly concerned with finding the point of view that allows him best to avoid the exaggerations and misfocusings of his own varying vision.

The first production of *Andorra* took place in the year Frisch reached the age of fifty, and it achieved a new height in his influence. *Andorra* was a turning point; we still do not know in what direction the new road will lead him.

Frisch's divorce in 1959 also resulted in a change in his personal life. To this divorce we perhaps owe the beautiful novella *The Couple* (1962). This novella, in which the contemplative tone is so dominant that we might more correctly speak of it as an essay, is the story of two people who seem to be leading a life like that which Frisch himself, because of incompatibility and growing older, had renounced. In his picture of an anonymous married couple, Frisch illuminates the theme of marriage from all angles, taking pains to find justification for its lasting until the death of one or the other of the partners.

The Couple is not a judgment against marriage as a "prison" or a "coffin of love," but neither does it suggest that one should finally resign himself to marital status as an institution that has existed from time immemorial. But again this does not mean that Frisch acknowledges marriage as a "divinely ordained institution" (as did his contemporary Thomas Mann), a concept that would definitely not fit into Frisch's philosophy. Marriage here appears as a protective covering, necessary and therefore also good. It is hardly different from clothing and shelter, which are also necessary to man, and just as subject to wear. The "two-ness" that becomes a habit between the two "love-dead" bodies need not lead to unfeeling estrangement. It may instead lead to a tensionless state between the mates, so that the marriage becomes merely a contractual agreement in which even the presence of a child makes no basic difference. And only through the death of one can the twofold form of living give way to a new, almost liberating dynamic, a change, the tension of which may release new intellectual powers. "The past is no longer a theme, the present is weak because it erodes from day to day, the future means getting old in any case. The adventure of being a couple takes place when you no longer are one, because one of you was operated on too late, or killed in an airplane accident."

The forms in which Frisch anticipates death are typical: as an attack from the outside, perhaps even the result of one of the thousands of catastrophes our technological age holds in readiness. The story presents eternal thoughts through the medium of events conditioned

by the times, as do *I'm Not Stiller* and *Homo Faber*.
In this small, closely woven piece of prose Frisch's creative originality comes impressively into play.

Can this also be said of his next major work, the
novel *A Wilderness of Mirrors* (1964)? With it Frisch
has enriched German-language literature with a kind of
picaresque novel that throws rays of cryptic humor on
the everyday life of our times. As in *I'm Not Stiller* and
Homo Faber, we are dealing once again with a tale of
ego-identity—that is, with the narrator, who sacrifices
his recognized identity in order to achieve a true identity. To have another life, he imagines:

a man has had a mishap, for example a traffic accident, his
face is cut, there is no danger to his life, only the danger
that he may have lost his eyesight. He knows this. He lies
in the hospital for a long time with his eyes bandaged. He
can speak. He can hear: birds in the park outside the open
window, sometimes planes, then voices in the room, the
quiet of night, rain in the early morning. He can smell:
applesauce, flowers, disinfectants. He can think whatever
he wants to, and he thinks. . . . One morning the band-
age is removed, and he realizes that he can see, but remains
silent; he does not say that he sees, to no one, ever. . . .
His life from then on, in which he plays the blind man,
even when only one other person is present; his relations
with people who do not know that he can see; his social
possibilities, his vocational possibilities that come about
because he never says that he sees; life as a game, his freedom thanks to a secret, etc.

He imagines: his name might be Gantenbein.

Once again Frisch allows a character to slip into
new garments in order that he may be able, even though

illegally, to live more legitimately in his own eyes. Life is only possible and worth living if you continually outwit it. For standardization and bureaucracy have become so predominant, are so effective in ruling all forms of social life, that the meager elbowroom that remains does not allow people to deploy their talents. Arbitrary action thus has become the only way to step out of his social dilemma, which, of course, always includes a risk. It can lead the individual easily into a clash with the law (that is, reality), and that is why another skin has quickly to be donned.

Gantenbein is willing to take this risk and become a different personality. What Stiller did not entirely succeed in doing, Gantenbein now manages to do. An "I" is freed from its old self and assumes the role of a blind man—a blind man who sees. The narrator says that Gantenbein will build his life on acting as if he believes what people tell him, and he will experience world events as they are presented in the newspapers. For people, generally, want their fellow humans as gullible and naive as Gantenbein is now going to appear to be, and in doing so he will become all the more popular. "He will meet a gentleman who has just lectured about the freedom of culture and will ask whether another gentleman, who played a leading role under Hitler, is also in the room, not seeing that it is the same man." The novel offers, with fine impartiality, a critique of the times, revealed in all the phases and situations through which the blind man passes. The blind man is also able to assume personal responsibility for the sins others have committed and for which they feel no guilt.

But Frisch does not settle for only one variation of changed personality. He often changes the personality of one fictional character several times in an attempt to show the human tendency of most people to present to their surroundings more than just one facet of their personality. Gantenbein says, " 'I try on stories like clothes.' " Each personality also has a name: married to the actress Lila, Gantenbein is also, simultaneously, Enderlin, another part of the manufactured personality, who helps make Lila's experiences as a woman more varied and complete.

But neither does Lila always remain Lila. Through the wild profusion of Gantenbein's imaginings, she is now the wife of an architect, now an Italian contessa, now a woman physician, now a mother. Reality and fantasy overlap continually in this novel; we get to see not just one world, but each world as seen through the temperament of each personality Gantenbein assumes. All these worlds, as they are disclosed to us, are finally spread like a fan, the expanding psyche of the protagonist. In the process, the protagonist is gradually unmasked as one who fools the world, laughs at it, feels himself superior to it, but at the same time lives at its expense. "Gantenbein is happy that he is not really blind." Can we quite believe what he claims are the underlying motives for the game he is playing? Gantenbein hopes that "people will not trouble to disguise themselves in front of a blind man, so that one can learn to know them better, and the result will be a truer relationship, in which one will accept even their lies, a relationship of greater mutual trust."

Like magic lantern slides, an infinite number of typical happenings and phenomena of our times appears before us, and the figures move close enough to touch. Whether it is the clerk who sells Gantenbein the glasses worn by the blind, or the doctor at the clinic, or the customs official handling the inspection of passengers' baggage, Frisch succeeds in capturing convincingly, with a few strokes, the everyday people of our time. Such mastery of literary technique is impressive. But it also lies at the edge of danger.

In this novel a narrating "I" reports life as a game. At the end of *A Wilderness of Mirrors*, "everything is as if it had never happened." This novel is a collection of the narrator's fantasized experiences, and, as in all of Frisch's fiction, the protagonist in all his personas is a reflection of the writer himself. "A man has had an experience, and now he looks for the story of that experience." Since Frisch has an extremely inventive and imaginative mind, experiences, more or less automatically, turn into art. Gantenbein puts forth countless blossoms. Once he is even transformed into an "I" who sees. But this voyage makes him aware of how much more desperate his real existence is, how dubious is human existence in general. When he returns to "being blind," he realizes with still greater clarity, how much better it is to continue to live as a blind man.

But each life, even when played as a role, contains hardship. The role cannot stop the process of aging, though it can, at best, conceal it a little. How clearly Frisch's features show through the Gantenbein-Enderlin mask when he says that the pace of a man of fifty becomes shorter, that his motions no longer involve the whole body, though this is to the benefit of his face, which becomes more personal from year to year, more expressive as he grows older. Old age has its advantages and disadvantages. Among its bitter disadvantages is to be too much respected—respected yet not loved a great deal by the younger generation. The young see the old as pathetic, even tiresome. And what, does Frisch think, will be the older man's reaction to all this? "He still will admire in order not to appear envious, and (in reality) he will be envious of everything he himself once had, envious because to him it no longer seems worth striving for."

Frisch's pessimism, which shapes his view of himself, is seen here. Having reached the meridian of life, he does not feel at all like a conqueror, even though he has accomplished something and enjoys the recognition of the world. All credit to the man who understands how to outwit life, who is able to create a small cosmos within himself, who can spin out of himself so many personalities that he finally no longer is sure which is the original.

Even Frisch's relationship to women, seen from this point of view, becomes basically dualistic, tragicomic. A man, he thinks, stresses either the tragic or the comic in his eroticism, according to his inclination as well as to the circumstances of the love affair. Frisch has an almost Freudian attitude toward the other sex when he says that what puts men into bondage to their wives is in the end nothing but their disdain for women, though most men do not admit this even to themselves.

Because of it they must exalt the women and pretend to be blind. If they follow the direction of nature, they rush to the next female, as though she were not also a woman, and they cannot give up their dreams. The more gallantly a man acts, the more scorn he has to hide.

Even this puzzling statement is probably born from experience. And out of experiences turned into inventions, the story or, to speak more correctly, the stories gush forth. A *Wilderness of Mirrors* contains a wealth of notions that at times seem to appear, almost independent of the author. Their independence, however, is deceptive. Frisch's mastery of composition prevents even one of the countless episodes from ever losing its relationship to the core. Language here is an instrument that Frisch commands with the greatest virtuosity, and the reader is likely to suspect at times that some of Gantenbein's escapades arise less from the compelling necessity of fate than from Frisch's pleasure in allowing his virtuosity free play. Also, in sharp jumps the language sometimes descends to the level of journalism, which is not like Frisch's language.

In a newspaper interview about A *Wilderness of Mirrors,* Frisch indicated how strongly the element of play influenced the conception and execution of this novel. Even when naming the protagonist, he yielded to a fanciful whim. In the same vein the fate of the protagonist is frequently developed through a torrent of playful inspirations, not all of which are of equal profundity.

Actually Frisch's A *Wilderness of Mirrors* is picaresque more in its superficial course of action than in its substance. For Gantenbein's "pranks," unlike those of Till Eulenspiegel, are not naive. Consciously willed, they originate entirely from the intellect.

Perhaps it is this lack of naiveté that leaves us with an ambivalent impression of the novel. Between what seems to have been hovering in Frisch's mind and what he succeeded in doing, there seems to be a gap. To me it appears to be more than merely Frisch's skeptical reservation toward what he has created when, toward the end of the novel, Gantenbein says: "I am blind. I don't always know it, only sometimes. Then I doubt again whether the happenings that I see in my mind are my life after all. I don't believe it. I cannot believe that what I see is really the way of the world." When looked at in this way, the protagonist of the novel is judging his creator, as it were, and the rascal's mask falls off. The game is over, and we realize that it was only a game. But I would have liked to have taken it more seriously.

Frisch's most recent drama, *Biography,* appeared in 1967 and has since been presented in most of the well-known German-language theaters. It appears to be related to his quasi-picaresque novel. In this play, which Frisch subtitled "A Game," he once more sought to conjure up the surrender of an individual's accepted personality. This time it is Dr. Kürmann, a researcher in psychology, who, having arrived at the peak of his life, hits upon the idea of finding out how he could have led his life differently. In order to arrive at an identification with his true self, he begins to observe himself from the outside. The spectator is given an opportunity to watch how he slips into another skin, even into several other skins as Gantenbein did.

Kürmann's method is to unwind his life skein backward to a decisive point in his development, and then to rewind it again in a way different from the life he had actually lived. But soon he has to recognize that this second living out of life, which the spectator becomes an eyewitness of—that is, trying out other possibilities of life on another level—does not lead to a more satisfying, much less a happier, end than his previous life. Life is always and everywhere full of dangers, traps, deficiencies. Nothing awaits him at the end of his alternate life but death by cancer, the plague of our century. At this point, therefore, Kürmann voluntarily rejects his fantasy life. Back to his real life, he reconciles himself to the fact that his wife has a lover and even welcomes him into his home.

This somewhat overworked theme of Frisch's, the exploration of how far a man can deviate from the lines determined by his nature and development and whether he should make the attempt at all, even when life is most burdensome to him, may have received its final treatment in *Biography*. The whole complex of questions is terminated by an unmistakable no—unless we are ready, along with the sacrifice of our real identity, to accept annihilation, death in the attempt.

Frisch himself says of the play that it was meant as a comedy, in the sense of the classical definition: a play in which a serious subject is presented lightly. This many-faceted work, rich in nuances, also touches in parts the magic circle of tragedy. *Biography*, though entertaining, at times even amusing to its reader or spectator, is tragic because of its acknowledgment that nobody is allowed to live life twice. That may be the reason why Frisch has his protagonist, Dr. Kürmann, experience his "second" life in the form of a theater rehearsal. Theater on theater, an imagined, artificial happening on stage, i.e., at a place—the only place!— where second and even more realities can come true, is the final effect that Frisch's development has thus far led to. Renunciation of portraying reality, as well as of a mere scene of a parable, has become the distinguishing mark of Frisch's play *Biography*, a clearcut picture of an end of a line of development.

Frisch, a man who this year has entered his sixties, has come, no doubt, to a crossroads. We cannot predict the direction he will enter upon. Asked in April 1971 whether he was planning or writing a new novel or another drama, he said no. His next book to be published would probably be another diary, he said, covering the years 1966–1969, a general review of a period parallel to the one between 1946 and 1949 and, hopefully, as interesting, deep, and elucidating as was the *Diary 1946–1949*.

Bibliography

The date immediately following an English title indicates
the date of translation; if no date follows the English title,
no English translation of that work has been published.

1. Works by Max Frisch

Afterthoughts to Don Juan. *Don Juan: Nachträgliches zu
   einem Stück*, in *Ausgewählte Prosa*, 1967.
Andorra, 1962. *Andorra*, 1962.
Answer from Silence. *Antwort aus der Stille*, 1937.
Bin, or The Journey to Peking. *Bin, oder Die Reise nach
   Peking*, 1945.
Biography: A Game, 1969. *Biographie: Ein Spiel*, 1967.
The Chinese Wall, 1961. *Die chinesische Mauer*, 1947.
Count Öderland, 1962. *Graf Öderland*, 1951.
The Couple. *Das Paar*, in *Jahresring*, 1961–62, Deutsche
   Verlags-Anstalt, Stuttgart.
Diary with Marion. *Tagebuch mit Marion*, 1947.
Diary 1946–1949. *Tagebuch 1946–1949*, 1950.
The Difficult Ones. *Die Schwierigen, oder J'adore ce qui
   me brûle*, 1943.
Don Juan, or The Love of Geometry, in *Three Plays*, 1967.
   Don Juan, oder Die Liebe zur Geometrie, 1953.
The Firebugs, 1959. British translation, *The Fire Raisers*,
   1962. *Biedermann und die Brandstifter*, 1953.
The Great Rage of Philip Hotz, in *Three Plays*, 1967. *Die
   grosse Wut des Philipp Hotz*, 1958.

Homo Faber, 1959. *Homo Faber*, 1957.
I'm Not Stiller, 1958. *Stiller*, 1954.
Jürg Reinhart. *Jürg Reinhart*, 1934.
Leaves from a Knapsack. *Blätter aus dem Brotsack*, 1940.
Our Arrogance toward America. *Unsere Arroganz gegenü-
ber Amerika*, in *Öffentlichkeit als Partner*, 1967.
Plays. *Stücke*, 2 vols., 1962.
(See individual titles for information about translations.)
The Public as Partner. *Öffentlichkeit als Partner*, 1967.
Reminiscences on Brecht. *Erinnerungen an Brecht*, 1968.
Santa Cruz. *Santa Cruz*, 1947.
Selected Prose. *Ausgewählte Prosa*, 1967.
They Are Singing Again. *Nun singen sie wieder*, 1946.
Transit. *Transit* (a film scenario), 1967.
When the War Was Over, in *Three Plays*, 1967. *Als der
Krieg zu Ende war*, 1949.
A Wilderness of Mirrors, 1965. *Mein Name sei Ganten-
bein*, 1964.

2. Works about Max Frisch

Bienek, Horst. "Werkstattgespräch mit Max Frisch." In
Werkstattgespräche mit Schriftstellern. Munich, 1962.
Bradley, B. L. "Max Frisch's *Homo Faber*: Theme and
Structural Device." *Germanic Review*, No. 41 (1966).
Davison, Dennis. "Max Frisch's *The Fire Raisers*." *Kos-
mos*, No. 1 (1969), pp. 147-57.
Falkenberg, Hans-Geert. "Leben und Werk Max Frischs."
Blätter des Deutschen Theaters in Göttingen, No. 110
(1956-57).
Hagelstange, Rudolf. "Verleihung des Georg-Büchner-
Preises an Max Frisch: Rede auf den Preisträger." In
*Jahrbuch der Deutschen Akademie für Sprache und
Dichtung*. Darmstadt, 1958.
Hammer, J. C. "The Humanism of Max Frisch: An Ex-

amination of Three of the Plays." *German Quarterly*, No. 42 (1969), pp. 718-26.

Harris, K. *"Stiller:* Ich oder Nicht-Ich?" *German Quarterly*, No. 41 (1968), pp. 689-97.

Hoffmann, Charles W. "The Search for Self: Inner Freedom and Relatedness in the Novels of Max Frisch." No. 113 (1969), pp. 91-113.

Pickar, Gertrud B. *"Biedermann und die Brandstifter:* The Dilemma of Language." *Modern Languages*, No. 50 (1969), pp. 99-105.

Stäuble, Eduard. *Max Frisch, Gedankliche Grundzüge in seinem Werk.* Basel, 1967.

————. *Max Frisch, Gesamtdarstellung seines Werks.* Sankt Gallen, 1967.

Whyte, A. "Labyrinths of Modern Fiction—Max Frisch's *Stiller* as a Novel of Alienation and the 'Nouveau Roman.' " *Arcadia*, No. 2 (1967), pp. 288-305.

Index

113